Llewellyn's Self-Improvement Series

HYPNOSIS

A Power Program for Self-Improvement, Changing Your Life and Helping Others

(formerly *Daydream Your Way To Success*)

William W. Hewitt

1989
Llewellyn Publications
St. Paul, Minnesota, 55164-0383, U.S.A.

International Standard Book Number: 0-87542-300-0
Library of Congress Catalog Number: 85-45283

First Edition, 1986
First Printing, 1986
Second Printing, 1987
Third Printing, 1987
Fourth Printing, 1989

Library of Congress Cataloging-in-Publication Data
Hewitt, William W., 1929–
    Hypnosis: a power program for self-improvement, changing your life, and helping others / William Hewitt.
      p.   cm. — (Llewellyn's self-improvement series)
    Rev. Ed. of: Daydream your way to succaess. 1st ed. 1986
      1. Hypnotism.   2. Success.   I. Hewitt, William W., 1929–
Daydream your way to success.   II. Title.   III. Series.
BF1152.H57   1987   87-35391
154.7—dc19   CIP

Cover Photo by Michael Tcherevkoff

Produced by Llewellyn Publications
Typography and Art property of Chester-Kent, Inc.

Published by
LLEWELLYN PUBLICATIONS
A Division of Chester-Kent, Inc.
P.O. Box 64383
St. Paul, MN 55164-0383, U.S.A.

Printed in the United States of America

All miracles start in the mind. Learn to use your mind to create your own miracles.

Everyone wants more out of life—to feel better, to realize self-fulfillment, to be happier and healthier, to know and understand more, to solve problems faster and easier, to become more successful, and so on. *Hypnosis* details exactly how to gain these things you want—to enrich your life at every level. No matter how simple or profound your goals, this book teaches you how to realize those goals and how to maintain that level of success once it is attained.

This book will teach you, in easy to understand and apply language, how to use hypnosis for yourself or others. The author gives complete instructions on how to hypnotize for weight loss, stopping bad habits, gaining self-confidence, becoming more efficient in your work, getting rid of phobias, poor self-image, sexual problems and much more.

Use the word-for-word routines for self-hypnosis or in helping others to attain their goals. Set up your own practice as a hypnotherapist once you are accomplished in the field. Make custom tapes for yourself, inserting whatever suggestions you need to attain your goals. Learn each step from this book and success is assured.

You experience a state of hypnosis every time you enter sleep. It is a natural phenomenon. *Hypnosis* teaches you how to use this natural state to achieve success in any endeavor you choose. This is not magic; it is a powerful key to unlock the magic within each of us.

About the Author

WILLIAM W. HEWITT has practiced clinical hypnosis professionally since 1972. He has his own practice in Colorado. He is actively involved in lecturing in the areas of hypnosis, psychic phenomena, mind control, and other subjects. He has also been a technical writer for the past 23 years in the areas of data processing, computers, mining, management procedures, medical equipment, and other fields of interest. Mr. Hewitt is a professional astrologer and a member of the American Federation of Astrologers. He is also a graduate of the Silva Mind Control basic and graduate courses. He uses self-hypnosis daily to enable him to quickly learn the technicalities and details needed for his technical writing assignments.

To Write to the Author

We cannot guarantee that every letter written to the author can be answered, but all will be forwarded to them. Both the author and the publisher appreciate hearing from readers, learning of your enjoyment and benefit from this book. Llewellyn also publishes a bi-monthly news magazine with news and reviews of practical esoteric studies and articles helpful to the student, and some readers' questions and comments to the author may be answered through this magazine's columns if permission to do is included in the original letter. The author sometimes participates in seminars and workshops, and dates and places are announced in *The Llewellyn New Times*. To write to the author, or to ask a question, write to:

William W. Hewitt
c/o THE LLEWELLYN NEW TIMES
P.O. Box 64383-300, St. Paul, MN 55164-0383, U.S.A.

Please enclose a self-addressed, stamped envelope for reply, or $1.00 to cover costs.

*This book is dedicated to all
men and women everywhere who do
their very best every day to make
the world a better place in which to live.*

Other books by William Hewitt

Beyond Hypnosis

Forthcoming books by William Heweitt

Tea Leaf Reading

Table of Contents

INTRODUCTION

Hypnosis is a lot like daydreaming. When you daydream, you alter your state of consciousness to the alpha frequency region and then engage in your fantasies. All the while, you are conscious and aware, yet you remain oblivious to external distractions. Daydreaming is a perfectly normal, safe, healthy phenomenon that we all engage in from time to time. Sometimes a person's daydreaming is so intense and so goal-oriented that the person actually causes the goal to be achieved. This usually happens spontaneously and without deliberate intent.

Hypnosis is a technique for enabling you to achieve this altered state of consciousness. . .the daydream state . . .deliberately and to direct your attention to specific goals so the goals will be achieved. Like daydreaming, hypnosis is a perfectly normal, safe, healthy phenomenon. In hypnosis, like daydreaming, you are conscious and aware, yet remain oblivious to external distractions. In both daydreaming and hypnosis your mind adjusts to the alpha frequency range (to be discussed in detail later). The difference is that in hypnosis your mind is directed to specific beneficial goals you wish to achieve, and not to fantasies as in daydreaming. Some beneficial goals might be: to quit smoking; to go on a diet; to improve your self-image; overcome phobias and fears; improve memory, etc. The list of uses is nearly limitless.

This book teaches you step by step to become a hypnotist. When you finish the book, you will know how to hypnotize others or yourself for any beneficial, worthwhile purpose. The book includes complete word by word hyp nosis techniques. Actual case examples are included to illustrate specific points. Nothing is left for you to wonder about. This book even teaches you how to modify the techniques in the book, and how to develop your own procedures.

If you want to learn hypnosis as part of a get-rich-quick scheme or to exercise control over others, *forget it!* This book does not tell you how to do those things.

However, if you want to expand your awareness, reshape and enrich your own life or the lives of others, and do so in a spirit of brotherhood and love, then read on.

Hypnosis is one of the most valuable tools in the world today for the enrichment of lives. With hypnosis, undesirable habits can be broken. . .desirable habits can be created. . .every sort of human problem can be dealt with constructively and resolved. . .true happiness can be instilled to replace unhappiness. The list goes on and on.

Why, then, isn't everyone engaged in daily self-hypnosis? Lack of education and knowledge are the main reasons. Most people lack good information, but possess a great deal of misinformation. There are few places to turn to for the knowledge. It isn't taught in public schools. Only a handful of colleges even have courses in hypnosis, and many of these are superficial. A few commercial schools offer hypnosis, frequently at inflated prices.

Thirteen years of first hand knowledge, training, and experience are packed into this book in a simple, lucid, and yet detailed presentation. This is a HOW TO book, and I leave no stone unturned in presenting everything you need to know to master hypnosis and self-hypnosis. If you want to learn just for your own edification, it is here. If you want to become a professional and go into business either full time or part time, it is here. If you want to develop the skill to help others, it is here. If your intent is regression, it is here. If you want to learn to develop your own hypnosis techniques, it is here.

All you need to understand this book and master hypnosis is average intelligence and the ability to read. That's all! No college degree...no high school diploma...no super intelligence are needed. In fact, this book will tell you how to start developing your own super intelligence.

This book strips away the shroud of mystery and ignorance that has cloaked hypnosis for centuries. What is left is a beautiful, powerful, simple, and natural skill for enriching the lives of all who embrace it.

To the best of my awareness, no other book on the market approaches the subject of hypnosis in the depth, in the specifics of procedures, and in the spirit of humanity as does this book.

Profile of the Author: I have been a practicing hypnotist for over 12 years, and have hypnotized many hundreds of people in just about every conceivable situation.

The first four years I practiced part-time on weekends and in the evenings with no charge to my subjects. I earned my living in employment to corporations as a technical writer. I am an altruistic person, and hypnosis gave me the chance to help others.

The demands on my time became so great that I decided to go into hypnosis full time as a business. This was a professionally satisfying success. Financially I made an adequate living for a while (I'll expand on this in a moment). At the time, I charged $25 per session which was $10 to $25 per session less than most other hypnotists were charging. I have a fanatical dislike for greed which explains my lower fees. Nonetheless, in spite of high expenses (rent, advertising, phone, etc.) I did quite well.

Then two events happened within a few months of each other that destroyed the hypnosis market in my metropolitan area. Two hypnotists (one a physician, the other a psychologist) were indicted in criminal charges in non-related cases. The physician was found guilty of massive and flagrant misuse of hypnosis for personal gain to the detriment of his patients. His medical license was revoked, but there was no jail sentence imposed.

In the case of the psychologist, I was the one who filed the initial charges against him with the state attorney general's office. The ensuing investigation revealed that I had only seen the tip of a huge, ugly iceberg. He was sentenced to eight years in prison.

The media coverage of these two cases was massive. There was a liberal amount of yellow journalism thrown in, so that all hypnotists were tarred with the same brush. The result was that it was nearly impossible to earn a dime as a hypnotist for quite some time.

So I went back to technical writing for a living while practicing hypnosis on the side once again. To this day, this is what I am doing. Occasionally I charge a fee of $35 per session (plus travel expense where applicable), but for the most part I do not charge.

My purpose in writing this book is to present hypnosis as the honorable, beneficial skill that it is. Whether you practice self-hypnosis in the quiet solitude of your room or practice with a loved one or friend, the benefits can be enormous. A husband and wife can be drawn closer together in love, harmony, and understanding than they ever dreamed possible just by practicing hypnosis together for common goals. In self-hypnosis, you can be drawn closer to your own higher self and through that higher self to all others. And there really are no negative aspects to hypnosis. If you approach it with integrity, you reap beneficial results. If you approach it lackadaisically, you have lackadaisical results.

In the first 11 chapters I explain what hypnosis is, how it works, and how you can master the art of hypnosis. Then comes the frosting on the cake: Chapters 12 and 13. Chapter 12 is devoted entirely to self-hypnosis...how you can do it to yourself, unaided, any time you desire for virtually any purpose you desire. The power, scope and uses of self-hypnosis can blow your mind. . .blow it into new, heightened levels of awareness and achievement. Then in Chapter 14 we go "beyond hypnosis" into the exciting area of psychic phenomena, astral world, telepathy, etc.

Understanding this brief profile of me should enhance your understanding of the contents of this book. This book is unique as hypnosis books go, and knowing where I am coming from explains why.

Now turn the page and begin reading, enjoying, and learning a new and valuable skill. This may well turn out to be one of the most beneficial experiences of your life to date.

William W. Hewitt

CHAPTER 1

HOW TO BE A HYPNOTIST

Nearly everyone can quickly and easily learn the techniques for hypnosis and become a hypnotist. However, to be a good hypnotist is something else again.

To be a good hypnotist you need to have integrity, honesty, dedication, and must really care about all humanity. Assuming you have these personal qualities, then all you need to do is memorize the techniques. Then just practice, practice, and more practice. And learn each time you practice. Then you will be able to call yourself a hypnotist.

Hypnosis is a tool to enable you to improve yourself or anyone else in any manner desired. This book will teach you step by step how to do just that. The first 11 chapters teach you to be a hypnotist for benefit, enjoyment, enrichment, and even profit. Chapter 12 brings it all together in how you can improve the quality of your life all by yourself using self-hypnosis. Chapter 14 takes a brief look at things "beyond hypnosis."

In this first chapter, we will explore the subject of hypnosis in general. I'll explode a few myths about hypnosis, give a few do's and don'ts, and tell you how to do your initial counseling with a subject.

In chapters 2 through 6, I will take you through six consecutive hypnosis sessions exactly as I do with a client for the purpose of *diet control*. The actual hypnosis procedures are printed out in full so you can use them. I chose diet control because it makes use of most of the types of procedures you need. Also, diet control is currently a popular subject.

Chapter 7 discusses using hypnosis for regression (past lives) which seems to be a current interest also. I include the procedure I have used quite successfully.

Chapter 8 is a collection of hypnotic suggestions for just about every purpose you are likely to encounter.

Chapter 9 is a potpourri chapter. Here I discuss things that didn't fit well into other chapters. Things like hypnotizing children, group hypnosis, and stage hypnosis.

Chapter 10 is a collection of some case histories to augment those given in the other chapters. The cases selected are those that illustrate some specific point about hypnosis.

Chapter 11 contains some additional hypnosis routines for specific purposes to augment the many routines delineated in the other chapters.

Chapter 12 deals exclusively with self-hypnosis. How you can do it to yourself, all by yourself, and achieve virtually any goal, be it material gain, spiritual gain, healing of wounds, overcoming illness, changing habits, etc. This chapter really brings the first 11 chapters into sharper focus for you.

Chapter 13 contains detailed instructions for a broad spectrum of practical everyday applications.

Chapter 14 contains two things: a brief summary of the entire subject, and a brief glimpse "beyond hypnosis" into the area broadly defined as psychic phenomena.

Definition of Terms

There are several terms that need defining because I use them many times throughout the book.

Operator: The word operator refers to the hypnotist, the one who is actually performing the hypnosis routines.

Subject: The word subject refers to the person who is

being hypnotized. This may also be referred to as the client.

Gender: If I am referring to a specific case history, I use the appropriate gender: i.e., he or his for a man, and she or her for a woman. If I am speaking illustratively, I almost always use she or her. Occasionally I use he/she to indicate either gender is applicable. Even when I use just the female gender, the situation could equally apply to a male. The reason I use female gender the most is because 90% of my subjects have been female. In my experience, women have been more open minded and receptive to hypnosis than men have been.

What Is Hypnosis?

By now you have probably gotten the idea that hypnosis is a daydreamlike state. In this state, the person's conscious mind becomes quiet or passive. This bares the subconscious mind so the hypnotist can introduce suggestions into the powerful subconscious mind.

Let's take a brief, slightly technical look at how the brain operates. The brain operates on frequency cycles that are measurable. These frequencies correspond to certain kinds of activity. Starting at the lowest frequency and working up, these are:

1. *Delta.* The frequency of brain activity ranges from 0 to 4 cycles per second. This is total unconsciousness. Not much is known about delta.

2. *Theta.* The frequency range is 4 to 7 cycles per second. Theta is part of the subconscious range and hypnosis can take place here, although very few people ever get down into the theta range for very long. All our emotional experiences seem to be recorded in theta. Theta is that special range that opens the door of consciousness to go "beyond hypnosis" into the world of psychic phenomena. This will be discussed briefly in the final chapter of this book.

3. *Alpha.* The frequency range of brain activity in alpha

is 7 to 14 cycles per second. Alpha is the range usually regarded as the subconscious range. This is where nearly all hypnosis takes place. This is also where all daydreaming takes place. Meditation is mostly in this range also, sometimes dipping into theta. Alpha is a very important region insofar as hypnosis is concerned, and it is mentioned in this book.

4. *Beta.* This is the conscious mind region with frequency ranges from 14 cycles upward. Beta is where we do our reasoning and conduct most of our affairs while awake. For the most part, we seem to operate around 20 cycles per second during most awake activity. At about 60 cycles per second, a person would be in acute hysteria. Above 60 cycles, I don't know what would happen . . . I suspect it wouldn't be pleasant.

When you go to sleep at night, your brain automatically cycles down from the beta range into alpha and then for brief cyclic periods into theta and delta. Most of your sleep is in alpha.

All hypnosis does is take advantage of this natural phenomenon. Hypnosis is a technique for causing the brain to cycle down into alpha without going to sleep. In alpha, the subconscious mind is open for suggestive input.

The conscious mind does not take suggestion very well. It is most useful for thinking, reasoning, and putting into action those things it already knows.

However, the subconscious mind is like an obedient slave. It doesn't think or reason. It just responds to what it is told. Herein lies the value and power of hypnosis. By hypnosis, you can pump powerful suggestions directly into your subconscious. Your subconscious accepts them and causes them to become reality. In part, it does this by informing the conscious mind that there is new information to be acted upon. The conscious mind loves to act on what it already has, so it starts to act on this new information. In part, we really do not understand why hypnosis works and how the subconscious mind brings about results. We do know that it does work and works quite well.

Suggestions: The suggestions used in hypnosis are covered extensively in other chapters. Suffice it to say for now that it is extremely important that all suggestions given are positive, constructive, and beneficial. This is because the subconscious mind doesn't know the difference between a good suggestion and a bad one. The subconscious mind merely accepts what you give it and then acts on it.

I know of a man who used a certain slang four-letter word for defecation literally hundreds of times a day in his speech. Eventually, he convinced his subconscious that he wanted to defecate, and he developed chronic diarrhea.

So be very careful or your wording at all times while giving suggestions. Words are powerful, and your subconscious mind takes them literally.

Myths: There are many serious misunderstandings about hypnosis. Many of these misunderstandings have been promoted by B-grade movies that depict people being transformed into zombie-like creatures by some superpowerful mystic who says, "Look into my eyes!" While this may make for an exciting movie, it is 100% fiction and has no resemblance to the truth. I will explore some of the more common myths here and set the record straight.

1. A hypnotist has magical powers. This is completely false. A hypnotist is a very ordinary human being who has mastered the skill of utilizing suggestion to bring about desired results.

2. A person can be hypnotized and made to do things against his or her will. Absolutely false! First of all, no person can even be hypnotized against his or her will. The subject must be 100% cooperative in order for hypnosis to work. Secondly, no one under hypnosis can be made to do

anything they would not freely do if not under hypnosis. During hypnosis, the subject can choose to accept or reject any suggestion given. If a suggestion is given that really upsets the subject, he or she would likely come out of hypnosis immediately of their own choice, and leave.

3. Only weak-minded people can be hypnotized. Again false. The contrary is true. The more intelligent a person is, the easier it is to hypnotize him/her. In fact, in certain cases of mental debility, hypnosis is impossible. Nearly everyone who wants to be hypnotized, can be hypnotized. Only about 1% of the population cannot be hypnotized; some of these are because of mental deficiencies and some are for reasons we don't understand.

4. A hypnotized person is in a trance or is unconscious. Not true at all. Under hypnosis, the subject is quite awake and aware, extremely so. The subject has merely focused his or her attention to where the hypnotist directs it, and is oblivious to anything else.

5. A person can get stuck in hypnosis. This is completely false. Even if the operator dropped dead after putting the subject under deep hypnosis, the subject would come out of it quite easily. The subject would do one of two things: slip into a brief sleep and then awaken normally, or just open his or her eyes when the operator's voice had not been heard for some time.

6. Deep hypnosis is necessary for good results. Not true. Any level of hypnosis from light to very deep can bring good results.

Hypnotic State: Under hypnosis the person is very aware of where he/she is and what is happening. He/she hears everything around. The person is in a daydreamlike state of deep relaxation and often has either a numbness throughout the body or has no acute awareness of having a body.

Self-Hypnosis: It is possible to hypnotize yourself. I do it nearly every day and give myself constructive suggestions. It is much easier to hypnotize yourself if you have first been hypnotized by someone else and given the suggestion and instructions to do so. Very few people are successful at self-hypnosis without having been first hypnotized by someone else. This book will teach you how to teach yourself. I recommend you work with a partner who can hypnotize you so you can achieve the best possible results.

Going Into Business

Some of you may want to go into business either part time or full time. This brief section highlights some of the things you should consider in addition to the material covered in the rest of this book. Even if you have no interest beyond your personal use of hypnosis, you can gain from reading this section.

Things You Will Need:

1. A quiet office with a minimum of three chairs. One chair for you; a lounger chair for your subject; and a chair (optional type) for a third party. Clients frequently bring someone with them. If you have a room in your home that is convenient to use, it will save you paying high rent, and it also gives you a tax write-off. If you must rent an office, get one that is quiet, has ample parking, and has easy driving access from all directions.

2. A desk or table for writing.

3. A cassette tape recorder and a supply of blank tapes.

4. Paper, folders, and file space for record keeping.

5. A supply of printed self-hypnosis instructions (covered in chapter 3).

6. A supply of printed diet sheets (covered in chapter 3).

7. Two pen lights with fresh batteries. You need these

only if you read the induction procedures and the room is too dimly lit for reading.

8. A 6" x 6" card with a large, solid red dot drawn on it (covered in chapter 3).

9. All of your hypnosis routines typed up and handy for quick access in case you have a brief memory lapse.

10. Release forms. These are to be signed by your clients attesting that they understand the nature of hypnosis, enter it willingly, and release you from any guarantees or liabilities. Consult with your attorney about this.

11. Business cards.

12. Telephone.

13. Either a receptionist with an outer office or a recorder to answer your phone when you are giving an induction.

Expenses:

1. Rent (unless you work out of your home).

2. Advertising. This is expensive, but necessary to some degree. One display ad (perhaps 3 x 4 inches) in the Sunday newspaper is about as much as you need to spend. If you sign a long-term contract, you get lower rates. It is still expensive. A *must* is a small display ad in the yellow pages of the phone directory. I got 70% of my business from the yellow pages; 20% from word-of-mouth; 10% from the newspaper. This is large metropolitan area. I suspect that in smaller towns, you would get more from word-of-mouth and the newspaper and less from the yellow pages. This is a guess; I don't really know for sure.

Charges:

I charge (currently in 1986) $50 per session. A session lasts from 30 minutes to an hour. I do not go beyond one hour because I find that too much time in one session becomes counter-productive for the client. The charge includes everything . . . the tape recording, the self-hypnosis and diet handouts. If I make an office or house call, then I charge a modest fee for travel time and gasoline if it is over five miles one way.

In some parts of the country, a charge of over $50 per session might be reasonable (Westchester County, New York for example).

A charge of $15 to $20 per session might be more appropriate for small towns or rural areas.

My philosophy is that you charge the very least you can and still pay your expenses and give yourself a reasonable return for your time and skill.

My rule is to give a client the fewest possible sessions to achieve the desired goal. I never will allow a client to see me for more than six sessions. This is because I am building a client to be independent . . . to solve his/her own problems . . . and not be dependent on me. I teach the client self-hypnosis starting on the second session so he/she will have the tools to solve problems as effectively as I can.

I recommend you take a similar approach in your hypnosis practice. Don't get greedy. Think of your client's needs first. You will make out OK.

I do strongly recommend that you request payment *in advance* for each session. Once you give the session, you can't take it back if they don't pay or write a bad check.

You may want to give a price break incentive for pre-payment. For example, pay for five sessions on your first visit, and get the sixth one free.

I have only been beaten out of money once. It was by an advertising executive for whom I had helped to rid of a three-pack a day smoking habit. He wrote bad checks and refused to make them good. He was just one of those deadbeats one occasionally meets in business.

Miscellaneous Thoughts: Accept every invitation you can to speak at the Lion's Club (or any other club), at high school or college classes, house parties, or whatever. It is excellent advertisement.

If you can do so without disrupting family life, work out of your own home. You can keep your fees lower this way.

You may want to make house calls or office calls. A word of caution here . . . especially for women . . . be wary and alert. You never know what you may be getting into. There have been several times when I was called late at night to a rough part of town. I never had any trouble, but I rarely make house calls any longer.

How To Perform Hypnosis

First, you must either have the hypnosis routines memorized, or have them typed and handy so you can easily read them. This is covered thoroughly in other places in this book.

Next come a myriad of things to consider: tone of voice, pace of speech, where to position yourself and your subject, lighting conditions, noise conditions, background sounds, where to do it, should any sessions be recorded on tape, use of external equipment, what to observe in your subject, testing for results.

Tone and Pace: Just use the voice you were born with. That may sound like a stupid statement, but it really isn't. I have seen many beginning hypnotists deliberately try to alter their voices when performing to try to have a more resonant, deep, theatrical sound. This is nonsense. Whatever your normal speaking voice is, is just fine. A beautiful, melodic, resonant voice is certainly an asset, but it is by no means necessary. It is far more important that you know what you are doing and that you have a good rapport with and respect for your subject.

You do need to give some thought and practice to the pace of your speech. The speech pattern needs to be slow enough to give the subject time to respond to your directions and yet fast enough to retain her attention and her interest. If you go too slow, the subject's mind will most likely wander to other thoughts; you want to maintain the subject's attention to your voice. You will find that some people need a faster pace while others need a slower pace. Experience will help you find just the right pace.

A pause of two to five seconds is a good average. For example: "Relax your knees" (2 second pause) "Relax your calves" (2 second pause) "And now relax your toes" (1 second pause) "Relax your toes" (2 second pause).

In some visualization routines you may need longer pauses. For example: "I want you to imagine now that you are standing at the top of a spiral staircase" (3 second pause) "Create the staircase" (3 second pause) "It is carpeted. Create the carpet" (3 second pause). You get the idea.

Do not use your watch for timing these pauses; if you do you probably will get so concerned with time that you will lose track of what you are doing. Just develop a feel for the timing. When I conduct hypnosis, I perform the instructions myself as I give them, thereby keeping a comfortable pace.

Speak in a rather dull, monotonous voice. The idea is to bore the subject's conscious mind to the point that it stops being active, allowing the subconscious mind to be accessible and receptive to your suggestions. If there is too much inflection or drama in your voice, the subject's conscious mind tends to retain interest, thus remaining active and thwarting your goal of deep relaxation and susceptibility to suggestion.

Physical Positioning: I have performed hypnosis while sitting and while standing. I have had subjects who were reclining in recliner chairs, sitting in straight-backed chairs, lying in bed, lying on the floor, sitting cross-legged on the floor, and even standing. All positions work fine, but not necessarily for all situations. For example, a quick two-minute procedure to relieve pain works fine on a person who is standing up. But a thirty-minute procedure for diet control is out of the question for a person who is standing up.

Given a choice, the recliner chair or straight-backed, armless chair are the best for the subject. They are equally good. Both offer sufficient comfort and support, and the subject will rarely drift into sleep in either of these. I prefer my subjects to be in a straight-backed, armless chair. These are my personal preferences. As the operator, I also prefer a straight-backed, armless chair.

Lying in bed also offers comfort and support for the subject. The drawback here is that the subject might easily drift into sleep. This is because the body and mind have been conditioned every day that when you lie down, and your brain reaches alpha you go to sleep; this is the normal sleep process we all go through every night. A skilled operator can usually prevent this from happening. When you are working with bedridden people, this is the physical position you must deal with.

Lying on the floor has the same drawback as lying in bed. The subject is more likely to fall asleep. In addition, the floor tends to become uncomfortable rather quickly, so I do not recommend it for lengthy procedures.

Sitting cross-legged on the floor also tends to become uncomfortable rather quickly, so I do not recommend it for lengthy procedures. I use this position quite often myself for meditation (a form of self-hypnosis) and have had excellent results. I once was in deep meditation for 1½ hours in this position without having any physical discomfort. I doubt that an untrained, unskilled person could do that and still be able to get up, much less walk.

Typically, my subject will be in a recliner chair. I will be sitting in a straight-backed chair facing her. The distance between us might be from 2 to 6 feet. There may or may not be a table or desk between us; this isn't important one way or the other. Close enough so I can speak normally and be easily heard, yet far enough so as to not intimidate her. There are some procedures I use for special occasions that require me to stand immediately in front of the subject or even have physical contact with the subject. These are the exceptions, not the rule. In this book I will deal mainly with the most common methods and situations.

Ideally, the subject's chair should be placed so that no bright light falls on her eyes. Have windows (unless heavily draped) to her back. The same for electric lights . . . to her back. This makes it easier for her to relax and be comfortable.

Where To Conduct Hypnosis: Most anywhere works fine. I've operated in dimly lit rooms and in bright sunlight outdoors. I've operated in quiet and in noise. The ideal is a quiet, comfortable room with subdued lighting.

If unplanned distractions occur, use them to your advantage. Once I had just begun the hypnosis induction when a carpenter in the adjacent office began hammering nails in the wall right by my subject's head. It was a staccato bang, bang . . . bang. I quickly abandoned my usual induction routine and improvised. I said, "Outside noises will not distract you. In fact outside noises will help you to reach a deeper, healthier state of relaxation." Then as each "bang" occurred I said, "Go deeper" (bang) "deeper" (bang) "deeper and deeper" (bang), etc. My subject went into deep relaxation as though she was on a fast down elevator. I didn't even need to continue with the remainder of my planned routines. I immediately began giving the suggestions and then brought her out. The results were excellent.

What About Background Music: Many hypnotists regularly have soothing music or a special tape of the ocean's surf playing in the background while they perform the induction. I have tried both the music and the surf and found them to be satisfactory. However, I have just as satisfactory results without the background. I rarely use background music. It is just a personal preference. Try it both ways and see which you prefer.

Auxiliary Equipment: All you really need is an inexpensive portable AC/DC cassette recorder. I use this only to record one of the induction procedures while I am giving it. I then give the tape to the subject to keep. This is covered in a later chapter.

If you decide you want background sounds, then you will need the equipment for that.

Some hypnotists use an electric shock device to condition their subjects. For example, during the suggestion phase of the procedure the operator might say, "Imagine now that you are smoking a cigarette. Take a deep drag." (Then he would press the button and give the subject an electrical shock). This way the subject equates smoking to a painful experience. Result: he or she stops smoking. I am fanatically opposed to such procedures and devices. They can be dangerous and harmful. And they are totally unnecessary. A good hypnotist can achieve the same result without resorting to such unacceptable measures. I once took over an office that already had one of these machines. I refused to accept it as part of the inventory and wouldn't sign until it had been physically removed from the premises. My advice: AVOID ANY SUCH APPARATUS COMPLETELY. They are bad news!

Observing The Subject: The key items you look for are breathing patterns and muscle tone. As the subject slips into deep relaxation, breathing will be easy and rhythmic. There will be an occasional very deep breath with easy exhaling.

Watch the hands of your subject. Are they gripping the

arms of the lounger . . . fidgeting . . . twitching? Or are they resting without apparent tenseness.

The head should droop as the neck muscles relax. The jaw should slacken. There should be no signs of muscle strain or tenseness.

The eyelids may flutter. This is not tenseness but rather an indication that the subject is in a state called R.E.M., or rapid eye movement. This state occurs at about 10 cycles per second of brain activity which is well within the alpha range. So if you observe R.E.M. you know for sure that your subject is in hypnosis. The subject can be in hypnosis without R.E.M., so don't be concerned if you do not observe R.E.M.

In general, look for signs of relaxation to indicate that the subject is in hypnosis. Signs of nervousness or tenseness indicate she probably is not in hypnosis, or at most only on the edge of hypnosis.

Do not get overly concerned if a subject doesn't appear to be relaxing very much. No two people react exactly the same way to hypnosis. Just keep on executing routines; they will work in all but a few cases, as discussed earlier in this chapter.

I have had subjects who became as limp as dishrags within moments after I've started the induction. Others have figited through most of the first session before relaxing only slightly. A few really didn't start to relax until the second session.

I have had only one subject that I was unable to hypnotize. After three sessions, she was still as tense and high strung as a mouse walking through a room filled with hungry cats. I gave her a complete refund and sent her to a colleague. My colleague had the same unsatisfactory results.

The best indicator about the subject's responsiveness to hypnosis is to question her about it after you have brought her out of the hypnosis. The subject will tell you whether she was relaxed or not and exactly what she experienced. Of course, final results are the absolute indicator. If you are hypnotizing to stop smoking, and the subject stops, you know you performed your skill correctly and the subject was responsive.

Testing: Some hypnotists perform little tests during the induction to see if it is working. For example, they might tell the subject to try to raise her arm just after telling her "Your arm is like a log . . . stiff . . . immovable." If she raises her arm, she isn't under hypnosis yet. If she doesn't raise her arm, the induction has produced some level of hypnosis.

I do not do testing at all. My theory is that testing creates a doubt in the subject's mind. "Isn't he sure about what he is doing?" "Maybe I am not a good hypnosis subject?" "Will it work or not?" etc.

Even a more pragmatic view . . . what are you going to do if the test fails and she does raise her arm? The only thing you can do is continue the induction which you were going to do anyway.

My approach is one of confidence—the induction *does* work—and lo and behold, *it does.*

Pre-Hypnosis Consultation

The pre-hypnosis consultation usually immediately precedes hypnosis Session 1, which is covered in the next chapter. The consultation is extremely important and should not be skipped. NOTE: For self-hypnosis, a type of pre-hypnosis consultation is also recommended; this is covered in Chapter 12.

The purpose of the consultation is many-faceted. It is the time when you explain what hypnosis is to your subject and answer any questions that may arise. It gives you the opportunity to establish a rapport with the subject, gain his/her confidence, and have the subject perform several simple exercises to put him/her at ease. There are a number of key questions you need to ask the subject to determine whether or not you wish to proceed with the actual hypnosis.

If the subject is really apprehensive (after you have thoroughly explained the hypnosis program) about being hypnotized, *don't attempt to hypnotize her.* Ask her to think about it for a few days. Let her know that you will be happy to answer questions.

Conversely, if your subject wants to be hypnotized, but you have reservations about it, don't do it. It is vitally important that you and your subject have a mutual rapport and understanding if you are to have a successful program. Keep in mind always that the goal of hypnosis is to help someone gain more control over his or her life and to improve the quality of that life in some manner. This is difficult to achieve if there are obstacles standing between the operator and the subject. By obstacles, I do not mean physical barriers but rather non-physical barriers such as lack of trust, poor rapport, apprehension toward each other etc.

Do not hesitate to refuse hypnosis. Here is an example to illustrate the point. A woman came to my office to begin a series of six sessions for diet control. In our pre-hypnosis consultation, my sixth sense told me that something was seriously inharmonious between us. Under gentle questioning, the woman admitted a deep hatred and mistrust of men in general. She quickly said, "I won't allow that to interfere with anything though." Of course, I realized her good intentions weren't good enough. She needed help more with her hatred than with diet control, and only someone whom she had complete respect for could help her. So I refused to take her as a client. Instead, I set up an appointment for her to see a colleague, a female hypnotist, for consultation. The woman had a successful program with my colleague, conqueing both her hatred and her eating compulsion, and she phoned to thank me. No doubt she would have gone to the female hypnotist in the first place had she known about her. The point I want burned permanently into your mind is that you should always do what is best for the subject even if it deprives you of a fee or of an interesting experience.

IMPORTANT: If you suspect a mental problem or a health problem, do not attempt to deal with it. Refuse to take the person as a client until she has seen a physician and the physician sanctions the hypnosis treatment. Also, do not accept a client that you know or strongly suspect is on illegal drugs. The grief you can create for yourself can be a lifelong nightmare.

Consultation Scenario: The rough skeleton of the consultation should go something like this:

1. Have the subject fill out and sign a brief fact sheet that includes name, address, phone number, purpose in wanting hypnosis, name he/she prefers to be called, and any other data you may deem pertinent. I usually keep this brief, preferring to elicit the data from the subject during discussion and making my own notes.

2. Ask why she wants hypnosis. Take your time exploring this thoroughly. Frequently the reason given is not the real problem. If the answer is for diet control, find out what she has done in the past for diet. Does she have a health problem? Is she taking medication or drugs. . .what kind. . .why. . .is it under a doctor's care, etc. Do not leave this until you are comfortable with the answers. More discussion on this shortly.

3. Explain thoroughly what hypnosis is and isn't. Allay all apprehensions. Invite questions, Explain what your entire six session program is and what your fees are. Be sure to stress that there are no guarantees; the results

depend on her responsiveness. Stress also that she cannot be made to do anything under hypnosis that is contrary to her will . . . she cannot be made to do anything that she wouldn't be willing to do while not under hypnosis. Also stress that she will always be aware of everything that is happening and will remember everything that happened.

4. Give a mini-demonstration of two pre-hypnosis training exercises to show how simple hypnosis is. These two exercises are detailed a little later on in this chapter.

5. Then begin with Hypnosis Session #1.

The preceding five steps are a suggested outline for your consultation. In practice, you will develop your own style and sequence. The important things to achieve regardless of your structure are:

a. Inform the subject completely about you and hypnosis.

b. Inform yourself completely about the subject.

c. Establish a comfortable rapport between you and the subject.

Problem Areas: If the subject is under medical care, do not do anything to interfere with that. Unless you are a medical doctor (very few doctors know or practice hypnosis), do not play doctor; that is not your role and it could be detrimental to your subject. In cases where the subject has a medical situation, I always ask permission to consult with the subject's physician. If the subject says, "No," I do not do the hypnosis. If the subject says, "Yes," I then am guided by the results of my consultation with her physician.

———————————

Frequently the reason given for wanting hypnosis is

not really the problem that needs to be dealt with. Here is one of my cases that illustrates the point rather humorously.

Case: An attractive, middle aged woman came to me ostensibly for diet control. She didn't appear to me to have a weight problem, but I nevertheless went through a complete consultation with her explaining all about hypnosis and about my diet control program. After my explanation, she still was very apprehensive about hypnosis. So I continued questioning until she finally admitted that she was concerned that I would take sexual advantage of her while she was hypnotized. I assured her quite firmly, "You will be aware at all times, and I cannot make you do anything under hypnosis that you would not do willingly while not under hypnosis. She smiled weakly and muttered, *"That's the problem!"*

I no longer do hypnosis specifically for diet control, smoking, phobias, etc. I deal only with self-image improvement and handling of stress. I find these two items to be at the root of all problems. Of course, I may put in a suggestion or two about not smoking, or regulating appetite, but my main thrust is self-image improvement and/or stress control. I find that when one's self-image is healthy and balanced, problems go away or are handled satisfactorily.

Occasionally, bizarre things can happen and you must be ready to handle them in a calm, confident, mature manner. You must never let your subject think that you are not absolutely in command. You must never appear to be rattled, upset, confused, etc. And you must never scold the subject or express disappointment at their response. Whatever the subject does or says is the way it is, so you as operator must learn to accept that and deal with it

You must never, I repeat *never*, be judgmental. If the topic of abortion makes you see red, and you are a staunch anti-abortionist, do not attempt to help the young, unmarried girl who is experiencing deep guilt over having had an abortion. Your own feelings might well cause you to only intensify the girl's guilt rather than help her handle it.

If you forget what you are supposed to say while hypnotizing a subject, don't panic or stammer, or apologize. Just pause briefly and then say something like, "Just go on relaxing, deeper and deeper with each breath." In a moment, you will recall your lines (or find your nearby paper with the words on it). In the meantime, just improvise in a soft, slow, confident manner.

Here is the most bizarre situation I've encountered and how I handled it. A middle-aged woman burst into my office in hysteria. She was crying, screaming, and babbling incoherently. Fortunately, I had an hour until my next appointment. My wife, who was my receptionist, and I gently led her to one of my lounger chairs, and I asked her to sit down. I sat across from her and said nothing. I let her cry and babble until she was exhausted. In her babbling, I got enough of a story to know that she was suicidal and was en route to kill herself when she came to my office. The details of why she was going to kill herself aren't germane to this example. Just take my word that her life was a colossal mess. When she finally grew tired she said, "I'm sorry I have bothered you. I know there is no way you can hypnotize me or help me while I am in this condition," I said, "Let's just talk about it. Your eyes are all red; they must burn." She nodded yes. "Why not just close your eyes and rest them while we talk." She did, and I had her under hypnosis within minutes without her realizing it. My purpose was to get her to commit to herself under hypnosis to live for two more weeks while giving me a chance to help her. The story has a happy ending. After four sessions in two weeks, she had rejected the thought of suicide and had started to exercise her option to live. Over the subsequent weeks she very nicely restructured her life. That was in 1976. She is still alive and happy today.

———————

The bond between the operator and the subject grows very strong very quickly. Occasionally the subject either interprets that bond as something stronger and more personal, or else tries to become dependent on the operator.

Be forewarned that your subject may become infatuated with you. This is something you will have to handle in your own way. You must be firm without creating a feeling that you are rejecting the person. It is sound practice to not socialize with your subject . . . not even a casual luncheon date. When I've had an over-zealous subject try to get too familiar with me, I remind her that my wife is my receptionist. That has always thrown cold water on the situation. I highly recommend that if you are in this business, you have your husband or wife as the receptionist. If you are not in business, but are just practicing hypnosis as a hobby, try to have a third person present. Otherwise, you are on your own, and you may find yourself in an uncomfortable situation.

———————

Another problem that can grow out of this strong bond is that of dependency. As an operator, you use hypnosis to enable a person to become more independent; and this is nearly always the way it results. Once in a while, however, a subject finds it very comfortable to have the "strong, confident, all-knowing" operator to lean on. When this happens, you must wean them quickly for your sake as well as for theirs. Here is one situation I encountered that illustrates this.

Ms. X was a model who was fearful of virtually everything. She was the ex-mistress of a local mobster who was slain just minutes after she had left his house, so she feared for her life also. Both parents had been domineering while she was a youth. She was never allowed to make even the simplest decisions. Her parents told her what to do. Her agent told her what to do. Her mobster boyfriend told her what to do. She had never lived for herself. Her life was the stuff soap operas are made of. Then she came to me, and through hypnosis she learned how to be free. . .to live. . .to have courage. It was a great experience for her, and she didn't want to let go. After our six sessions were completed, she persisted in phoning me at the office during the day and at home every night. The first few times I was tolerant. Then I tried to politely tell her to stop phoning. Finally after about two weeks of futile attempts, I very coldly told her to never phone me again; if she did I would hang up and not talk. She cried, of course, but she mended quickly and went on to pursue a successful life on her own. She knew how, but didn't want to give up her security blanket. Sometimes you must take a firm stance for your subject's sake as well as yours. Another rule: Never allow your subject to get the upper hand or tell you what to do.

Do not allow unplanned responses to sidetrack you. Once I was hypnotizing a woman for the first time. At a point in the procedure I said "Your arms are now like logs. . . stiff. . .numb. . .simply immovable." She immediately broke into an ear-to-ear grin and began giggling. Her eyes remained closed, but she chuckled for a minute or so. I was curious as to why this was happening, but I ignored it. I just continued to monotonously speak the words to take her into deeper relaxation. Later, when the session was over she explained that her intent was to wave both arms vigorously in the air when I said they were immovable and loudly proclaim, "See, it's not working!" But she was unable to lift her arms. It struck her as silly that she could be aware of who she was, sitting unrestrained in the chair, and yet not be able to move her arms simply because I had said she couldn't move them. That explained her grin and giggling.

Pre-Hypnosis Exercises: Here are the two pre-hypnosis exercises I referred to earlier. Use them during your consultation period to familiarize your subject with hypnosis and put her at ease. The italicized words are the ones you say. NOTE: Self-hypnosis exercises are covered in Chapter 12.

Exercise 1: *I want you to close your eyes now for a brief exercise. I want you to picture a chalkboard in your mind. Create the chalkboard. It can be black or green or whatever color you wish. Create it. It has a chalk tray with chalk and an eraser in it. Do you have it?* (Wait for a response. When you get a yes response, proceed). *Fine. Now take a piece of chalk and draw a circle on your board. Do you have the circle?* (Wait for yes, then proceed). *Good. Now print the letter A inside the circle. Do you have A in the circle?* (Wait for yes, then proceed). *Now erase the A from inside the circle, but don't erase the circle. Say OK when you have done that.* (Wait for OK). *Very good. Now erase the circle and open your eyes.*

At this point you may have a brief dialog with the subject about her experience with the chalkboard. Assure her that whatever her experience was, it was fine. Each person responds differently. Some actually see the board. Others sense it. Others know intellectually that it is there. All responses are correct. There are no wrong experiences in hypnosis; whatever you experience is the way it is for you, and it is OK. Make a point of telling the subject that this sort of exercise happens frequently in hypnosis.

Exercise 2: *Close your eyes again for one more training exercise. Are you doing this? (Wait for yes, then proceed). Good. Keep your attention focused gently and casually on the tip of your nose and go on listening to the sound of my voice. In some of the hypnosis techniques we will be doing together, I will ask you to focus your attention on the tip of your nose in order to intensify your concentration and deepen your state of relaxation. If at any time during hypnosis you find your mind wandering, all you need to do is focus your attention on the tip of your nose as you are doing now and your mind will stop wandering and will once again follow my voice. Now you may open your eyes.*

You may have a brief dialog about this exercise, then you are ready to begin Hypnosis Session #1 as detailed in the next chapter.

CHAPTER 2

HYPNOSIS SESSION 1

Now we are ready to go through Hypnosis Session 1 exactly as I give it to my subjects. This session I use only the first time I hypnotize a subject. It is an excellent sequence of routines for testing a subject's responsiveness to the operator (you) and for getting the subject acclimated to the hypnosis procedures.

I have labeled each routine with a letter or a number/letter combination for easy identification. These identifying numbers, of course, you do not say to the subject. They are just for your records. In chapters that follow this one, I will use some of the routines that I have already given. In these cases, I will just say use routine **A** or **B** or whatever rather than repeat it word for word.

I recommend that you put each routine on a separate sheet of paper or a 4 x 6 inch card. This way you can arrange them in any order you want for any purpose. As you will see by the time you finish this book, you can create special procedures by putting a variety of routines in a desired order.

The routines that you say to the subject are in italics. It is good if you memorize them, but it is perfectly OK to read them. Initially, just memorize routine **A**. It is quite short, and when your subject sees you are speaking from memory, he tends to have more confidence in you. During routine **A** you have the subject close his eyes so from that point on he doesn't know if you are reading or speaking from memory. It really isn't that big of an issue anyway. You will find that you will have it all memorized anyway after doing it a few times. Having it all memorized does a lot for your confidence in yourself, also.

Session 1 consists of the sequence of routines as follows:

Session 1: A, 1A, B, 1B, 1C, 1D, 1E, 1F, 1G, 1H, 1J

Just before starting Session 1, I give the following brief instruction to the subject: *In a few moments I am going to ask you to close your eyes and follow my instructions. Shortly after we begin the session, I will ask you on three separate occasions to open your eyes. When I do ask, I really do not want you to open your eyes. I want you to pretend to try to open your eyes by stretching the eyelids, but I do not want you to open them. Then I will say something like, 'Now relax your eyes' at which time you may stop pretending to try to open them and just relax. Here is what I mean...* (at this point I demonstrate what I mean)...*now you try it* (I wait for a few moments to allow the subject to do with his eyelids what I just demonstrated). *That was fine. Of course, at the very end of this session I will really want you to open your eyes when I say something like 'In a few moments I will count from one to five and you will open your eyes and be wide awake.' Do you understand? In the beginning we will have three brief tests where I do not want you to open your eyes, but at the very end of the session I really do want you to open them.* (I wait for the subject to acknowledge that he understands. If he doesn't, I go over it until he does) *Now let's begin.*

Routine A

First I want you to stand up and take a good, complete stretch. Get all the kinks out. (I wait for a few moments while the subject stands up and stretches thoroughly) *That's fine. Now just sit in the chair and relax. Close your eyes and take a nice deep, full breath and exhale completely, all the way to the bottom of your lungs. All out. Do it again now. Just relax and let it all out. One more time, and this time hold your breath when you have filled your lungs with clean, refreshing, relaxing air. Hold it in. Keep your eyes closed. Now let your breath out slowly and feel yourself relaxing all over.*

Routine 1A
(Be sure to pause in between instructions)

Focus your attention on your knees now and relax everything below your knees. Relax your calves. Relax your ankles. Relax your feet. And relax your toes. Relax your toes. Everything below your knees now is loose and relaxed. Now relax your thighs as completely as you can. Let your thighs just droop limp and loose and heavy into the chair. Relax your hips and relax your waist. Now relax your chest as completely as you can. Allow your breathing to be easier and deeper, more regular and more relaxed. Relax your shoulders now. Let the muscles in your shoulders be heavy and loose. More and more completely relaxed. Relax your neck and throat. Let your head just droop as all the muscles in your neck just relax. Now relax your face as completely as you can. Allow your face to be smooth and loose, relaxed and easy, your jaws all loose and relaxed, your teeth are not quite touching. Everything smooth and loose and easy. Now relax as completely as you can all the little muscles around your eyelids. Feel your eyelids growing heavier and smoother. More and more deeply relaxed.

In a moment, I am going to ask you to open your eyelids. When I ask you to open them, your eyelids will be so relaxed and heavy they will just barely open and when I ask you to close your eyelids again you will allow yourself to relax even more completely. Now try to open your eyelids. Now close your eyes and feel yourself relaxing even more.

Routine B

I want you to imagine now that all your tensions, all your tightness, and all your fears and worries are draining away from the top of your head. Let it drain down through your face, down through your neck, through your shoulders, through your chest, your waist, your hips, your thighs, down through your knees, your calves, your ankles, your feet and out your toes. All your tension, all your tightness, all your worries and fears are draining away from the very tips of your toes, and you are relaxing more and more.

Routine 1B

We are going to do this relaxation exercise again. This time I want you to allow yourself to relax even more fully and completely than you did the first time.

Focus your attention on your knees once again and relax everything below your knees. Relax your calves. Relax your ankles. Relax your feet, and relax your toes. And now relax your thighs even more completely. Allow your thighs to droop limp and heavy into the chair. Relax your hips and your waist. Feel the relaxation flowing into your chest now. Relaxing the vital organs within your chest, your heart, your lungs, allowing your breathing to be more intense, more regular, more and more completely relaxed. Now relax your shoulders even more. Feel your shoulders heavy and loose. More and more deeply relaxed. Relax your neck and throat. Relax your face even more. Feel your face all smooth and loose, completely easy and relaxed all over. And now relax even more all the little muscles around your eyelids. Feel your eyelids heavy and smooth, more and more deeply relaxed.

In a moment when I ask you to open your eyelids, your eyelids will be so relaxed, so lazy, that they may not even work. But whether your eyelids open or whether they do not open, in either case, when I ask you to close your eyes again, you will allow yourself to relax even more completely. Open your eyelids. Now close your eyes, and feel yourself relaxing even more.

Routine 1C

We are going to do this relaxation exercise once again. This time I want you to allow yourself to relax completely. There is nothing to fear, you will always hear me, so just pull out all the stops and allow yourself to sink into perfect relaxation.

Focus your attention again upon your knees and relax everything below your knees. Relax your calves, relax your ankles, relax your feet, and relax your toes. Now relax your thighs completely. Feel the deep and heavy relaxation flowing into your hips now. Feel it going up through your waist, flowing into your chest, to your shoulders, heavy and loose, completely relaxed. And now this heavy relaxed feeling is going into your neck and throat, all over your face. Your face is all smooth and loose, completly easy and relaxed, and the heavy relaxation is flowing into your eyes and eyelids now. Your eyelids are so heavy and so smooth. Ever more deeply relaxed.

Routine 1D

In a moment when I ask you to open your eyelids, I want you to believe very, very strongly that your eyelids are glued together. I want you to imagine that your eyelids are one piece of skin. Like one piece of skin. Don't be antagonistic or skeptical and say that you can open your eyelids. Just believe, just imagine that your eyelids are glued together. And if you believe and if you imagine that you cannot open your eyelids, you will really not be able to open them. Believe now very very strongly that your eyelids are glued together. Imagine your eyelids are like one piece of skin. Now try to open your eyes. Now let your eyes relax. Feel yourself relaxing all over.

Routine 1E

I want you to imagine now that you are looking at a blackboard. And on the blackboard is a circle. Into the circle put an X. And now erase the X from inside the circle. And now erase the circle. Forget about the blackboard now as you just go on relaxing more and more deeply.

In a moment, I am going to count backward from 100. I want you to count with me silently to yourself. Say each number to your-self as I say it, then when I ask you, erase the number from your mind and allow yourself to relax even more deeply. 100. . .say the 100 to yourself. Now erase it from your mind and go deeper. 99. . . and erase it all away. 98 and erase it. 97 and now erase it so com-pletely there is nothing left at all, just deeper and deeper waves of relaxation.

Routine 1F

Focus your attention now on the very tip of your nose just as we practiced before. Keep your attention gently focused on the tip of your nose until you reach a point where your entire attention is on my voice. And when you reach that point, you can forget about your nose and just go on listening to my voice and allowing your-self to relax more and more deeply. And as you keep your attention focused very gently on the tip of your nose I am going to take you down through four progressively deeper levels of relaxa-tion.

Routine 1G

I will label these levels with letters of the alphabet, and when you reach the first level, level A, you will be ten times more deeply relaxed than you are even now. And then from level A we will go down to level B, and when you reach level B you will be ten times again more deeply relaxed than you were before. And from level B we will go down even further, down to level C. And when you reach level C you will be ten times again more deeply relaxed than before. And then from level C we will go all the way down to the deepest level of relaxation, level D. And when you reach level D, you will be ten times again more deeply relaxed than before. You are drifting down now, two times deeper with each breath that you exhale. Two times deeper with each breath. Your hands and fingers are so relaxed and heavy, and they keep growing heavier. Feel the

*heaviness growing in your hands and fingers. Heavy. . .heavier
still until now they are so heavy it is as though your hands and
fingers were made of lead. And this deep relaxed, heavy feeling is
flowing up through your forearms now. Feel it going up into your
upper arms. Flowing through your shoulders, into your neck, over
your face, over your eyes. Flowing up to your eyebrows, your
forehead, over the top of your head. The deep relaxed, heavy feeling
is flowing down the back of your head and down the back of your
neck. You are now approaching level A.*

Routine 1H
*You are on level A now and still going deeper. Five times
deeper now with each breath you exhale. Five times deeper with
each breath. Your mind is so still and peaceful. You're not thinking
of anything now. Too relaxed to think. Too comfortable to think.
And this heavy relaxation in your mind is flowing into your face
and eyes. It is flowing down through your neck and into your chest.
Flowing down to your waist, down through your hips, your
thighs, your knees, your calves, your ankles, your feet and your
toes. You are now approaching level B.*

Routine 1I
*You are on level B now and still drifting deeper. Floating
smoothly and gently into perfect relaxation. Your arms and legs are
so relaxed and heavy they feel like logs. Your arms and legs are stiff
and numb and heavy. . .simply immovable. Your arms and legs are
like planks of wood. You are now approaching level C. You are on
level C now and still drifting down. Sinking into the chair. Sinking
deeper and deeper into perfect relaxation. And as you go on drifting
even deeper, I am going to count backwards from 15 to 1. Each
number that I say will take you deeper and deeper still, and when I
reach 1 you will be on level D. 15, deeper, 14, deeper still, 13. .12. .
11. .10. .9. .8. .7. .6, let it all go now, 5. .4. .3 . .2. .1, so deep, so
dreamy, so heavy, so misty. You are now on level D now and still
drifting down. There is no limit now . . no limit. Go on floating,*

drifting deeper and deeper into perfect relaxation, deeper with each breath.

At this point you give your suggestions. If I am using this session as the only session I plan with a client, the suggestions will be as extensive as necessary for the problem being handled.

Usually this session is just the first of four or six planned for handling of a problem. In this case, I just put in a few general welfare suggestions such as:

1. *This is the first of a series of hypnosis sessions that will enable you to get more control of your life and to enrich your life by solving your problems.*

2. *Repeat the following statements to yourself as I say them: 'Every day in every way, I am getting better, better, and better.'*

3. *Positive thoughts bring me benefits and advantages I desire.*

You get the idea. You can use the above suggestions, or tailor your own. But you should put at least one suggestion in and probably no more than three at this point. Then proceed to the closing routine, 1J.

Routine 1J

The next time I see you, or whenever you hear my voice on tape, you will allow yourself to become ten times more deeply relaxed than you are now. And the suggestions I give you then will go ten times deeper into your mind.

In a few moments I will awaken you. When you awaken you will feel very relaxed and very refreshed all over. You will feel alive and alert, very refreshed. Full of energy. You will feel just wonderful. You will keep on feeling relaxed and fine all the rest of today, and all this evening. Tonight when you are ready to go to sleep, you will sleep like a log all night long. And the first thing you know it will be morning, and you will awaken feeling on top of the world.

I am now going to count from 1 to 5. At the count of 5 you will open your eyes, be wide awake and feeling fine, feeling relaxed, re-freshed, alert, and in very high spirits. Feeling simply terrific!

1...2...coming up slowly now...3...at the count of 5 you will open your eyes, be wide awake and feeling fine, feeling better than before...4...5. Here I usually snap my fingers at the count of 5 and say, *Open eyes, wide awake and feeling fine, feeling better than before, and this is so!*

Things to note about Session 1: Look over routines 1A, 1B, and 1C. At a quick glance, they seem to be the same. A closer look reveals subtle differences in the wording; these differences are very important. We progress from telling the subject to relax, to feel the relaxation, to you are now relaxed.

In routine 1J I have put in, "or whenever you hear my voice on tape." If you are not going to tape any sessions, you can leave this out. If you think you may be wanting to perform relaxation over the telephone, then also put in "or whenever you hear my voice on the telephone." The thing we are doing here is pre-conditioning our subject for future sessions.

CHAPTER 3

HYPNOSIS SESSION 2

In this session we really start to get down to business. We achieve two main goals: To begin specific routines and suggestions to deal with the diet and eating habits (or deal with whatever the problem is if not diet), and to begin teaching the subject self-hypnosis.

There are 16 routines, 14 of which are new. Routines **A** and **B** were detailed in chapter 2 and are not repeated here. Session 2 consists of the sequence of routines as follows:
Session 2: A, B, C, D, E, F, G, H, J, K, L, M, N, O, P, Q

Routine C
Focus your attention on your toes now, and allow your toes to relax completely. Each toe is loose and heavy. Now let this relaxation flow into your feet, into your ankles, your calves, your knees. Feel it flowing into your thighs, into your hips, into your waist, flowing up into your chest now. Feel your breathing easier and deeper, more regular and more relaxed. Now let the deep relaxed feeling go into your shoulders, down your arms, into your upper arms, your forearms, and into your hands and fingers, and flowing back into your forearms, your upper arms, your shoulders. Flowing into your neck, over your face, your chin, your cheeks, even your ears are relaxed. Feel it flowing into your eyes and eyelids

37

now. Your eyelids are so heavy and smooth. Flowing up into your eyebrows, over your forehead, over the top of your head, down the back of your head, and down the back of your neck.

Routine D

A new heaviness is starting in your toes now. Twice as heavy as the first time. Imagine a heavy weight on each toe. Feel the heaviness deep and even more relaxed. And this heavy, deep feeling is going into your feet, your ankles, your calves, your knees, going into your thighs, your hips, into your waist. Flowing up into your chest now, relaxing your heart, relaxing your lungs, allowing your breathing to be more intense, more regular, more and more completely relaxed. Now the deep heavy feeling is flowing into your shoulders, and down your arms, your forearms, into your hands and fingers. And now flowing back through your forearms, your upper arms, into your shoulders and into your neck. Flowing over your face, into your eyes, over your eyebrows, over your forehead, over the top of your head, down the back of your head and down the back of your neck.

Routine E

And a new heaviness is starting now at the top of your head. Twice as heavy as before. Twice as heavy. Imagine a heavy weight on the very top of your head, soft and relaxed and heavy. Feel the heavy relaxation flowing down into your face and eyes now, down through your neck, your shoulders, flowing down through your chest, your waist, your hips, your thighs, your knees, into your calves, your ankles, your feet and toes. Deeply relaxed, loose and limp, and comfortable from the top of your head to the very tip of your toes.

Routine F

I want you to imagine now that you are looking at a blackboard. On the blackboard imagine a circle. Into the circle we are going to place the letters of the alphabet in reverse order, and with each letter after you place it into the circle, you will erase it then from inside the circle and allow yourself to relax more and more deeply.

Picture the blackboard now. Picture the circle. Into the circle put the letter Z. Now erase the Z from inside the circle, and go deeper. Put Y into the circle, and erase it and go deeper. X, and erase it and go deeper still. W, and erase it. V, and erase it. U, and erase it. T, and erase it. S, and erase it. R, and erase it. Q, and erase it. P, and erase it. O, and erase it. N, and erase it. M, and erase it. L, and erase it. K, and erase it. J, and erase it. I, and erase it. H, and erase it. G, and erase it. F, and erase it. E, and erase it. D, and erase it. C, and erase it. B, and erase it. A, and erase it. Now erase the circle and forget about the blackboard. Just go on relaxing more and more deeply. Feel yourself sink into the chair, mind and body drifting deeper and deeper into relaxation, deeper with each breath.

Routine G

I want you to imagine now that you are looking at a clear, blue summer sky. And in the sky, a sky-writing airplane is writing your first name in fluffy, white cloudlike letters. See your name floating fluffy, white, and cloudlike in a clear, blue sky. Now let your name just dissolve away. Let the winds just blow your name away into the blue. Forget about your name. Forget you even have a name. Names are not important. Just go on listening to my voice and allowing yourself to relax more deeply.

Routine H

I want you to imagine now that I am placing on each of your knees a heavy bag of sand. Feel the sand pressing down on your knees. Your knees are growing heavier and more relaxed. In the sand is a very powerful numbing ingredient and the numbness is flowing down into your knees now. Your knees are growing numb and more numb under the sand. And the heavy, numb feeling is flowing down into your calves, into your ankles, into your feet and toes. Everything below your knees is numb and more numb from the sand. And now the heavy, numb feeling is going up into your thighs, flowing into your hips, through your waist, and into your chest. It flows into your shoulders, and they grow numb and heavy. It flows down your arms, your upper arms, your forearms, into your hands and fingers. Flowing back now through your forearms, your upper arms, your shoulders, and into your neck. Over your face, your eyes. Flowing up to your eyebrows, your forehead, over the top of your head, down the back of your head, and down the back of your neck.

Routine J
As you go on floating, drifting smoothly and gently, more and more deeply relaxed with each breath, I want you to focus your attention on the very tip of your nose. Keep your attention focused gently and lazily on the tip of your nose until you reach a point where your entire attention is on the sound of my voice. And when you reach that point, you can forget about your nose and just go on listening to my voice and allowing yourself to relax more and more deeply. As you keep your attention gently focused on the tip of your nose, I want you to imagine. . .imagine that I am placing on your tongue, in your mouth, a small bite of chocolate candy. You don't swallow it; it just sits there on your tongue. Notice the bitter taste of the chocolate. It is bitter and it is growing more bitter and more bitter as it just sits there, melting on your tongue. It is so bitter that you can hardly keep it in your mouth. It tastes terrible. From now on you will be completely free from any desire for chocolate or candy or sweet foods of any kind. You will be completely free from that desire, completely free from now on. I am taking the bitter chocolate from your mouth now. Your mouth feels clean now, all fresh and clean. You are glad that that ugly taste is gone from your tongue.

Routine K-1
(use only with female subjects)
I want you to imagine yourself. See yourself as you really

want to be, the real you. Alive and vibrant, in full control, serene and lovely. This is you. This is the real you. This is the woman you can really come to be. At this moment you are making yourself a promise. Not a promise to me...a promise to yourself...a commitment to become the real you. This commitment will be with you, stronger every day. From now on, every day you will become more and more completely the lovely woman you want to be. You will be relaxed and serene no matter what is going on around you. And anything that does happen, you can handle it in a relaxed and sensible manner. And you will feel so good, you will have all the energy in the world every single day. And it will be very easy for you to stay on your diet strictly every day. No matter where you are, no matter what you are doing.

Routine K-2
(use only with male subjects)

I want you to imagine yourself. See yourself as you really want to be, the real you. Confident and energetic, in full control, healthy and trim. This is you. This is the real you. This is the man you can really come to be. At this moment you are making yourself a promise. Not a promise to me...a promise to yourself...a commitment to become the real you. This commitment will be with you, stronger every day. From now on, every day you will become more and more completely the trim, handsome man you want to be. You will be relaxed and calm no matter what is going on around you. And anything that does happen, you can handle it in a relaxed and sensible manner. And you will feel very good, you will have all the energy in the world every single day. And it will be very easy for you to stay on your diet strictly every day. No matter where you are, no matter what you are doing.

Routine L

In the morning you will have a small serving or protein, a small serving of fruit or juice and one piece of toast without butter. For lunch you will have one small serving of protein and a small *serving of fresh fruit or vegetable. For dinner you will have a small dinner salad with a very light dressing, a small serving of protein and one half a cup of cooked vegetable served without butter or margarine.*

In routines where the word "prettier" is used, you may find it more appropriate to use "attractive." If the subject is a man, then use "handsome".

Routine M

You will always eat very slowly, and when you have eaten just a little of the proper sensible foods, you will feel full, completely full and satisfied on just a little bit of the right food. That is all your body needs right now. That is all you will want. You will have no desire at all for sweets or starches or rich greasy foods. The longer you stay on your diet the easier it will be and your weight will just melt away. All those extra pounds will just disappear so fast and so easy. Every day you will be smaller and lighter and prettier, and you will feel better and better every day. And you will also practice faithfully the little exercise in self-hypnosis that we are going to do together now.

Routine N

In a moment, I am going to ask you to open your eyes and look at a spot I am going to hold before you. You will not awaken when you open your eyes. You will not awaken. You will go even deeper into relaxation. Open your eyes now and look at the spot I am holding before you and take a deep, full breath.

When you told the subject to open her eyes, you should be holding up a card that has a large, bright red spot on it for her to direct her attention to. A handy size for this card is 6" x 6", preferably white card stock on which is drawn as large a circle as you can get on the card. The circle should be colored bright red. Hold the card at her eye level about 4 feet in front of her.

Deep and full. Now close your eyes, let your breath out and think 5 . . 5 . . 5 . . and go deeper. Again now, a deep, easy breath and think 4 . . 4 . . 4 . . and let it out. Again a deep breath, deep and full, think 3 . . 3 . . 3 . . and let it out. More and more deeply relaxed. Take in a deep breath and think 2 . . 2 . . 2 . . and let it out. Once more a deep breath, let it out and think 1 . . 1 . . let it all go now . . 1. Imagine now a heavy, deep force of relaxation just behind your eyelids. Feel this deep, relaxing force flowing down from your eyelids. Down through your face and neck, down through your shoulders and chest, your waist, your hips, down through your thighs, your knees, your calves, your ankles, your feet and toes.

Routine O

In a moment, I am going to count backward from 10 to 1. I want you to count with me silently to yourself. Think each number as I say it, and allow each number to take you deeper. 10 . . 9 . . 8 . . 7 . . 6 . . 5 . . 4 . . 3 . . 2 . . 1. You are now very deeply relaxed. You can give yourself the following suggestions. Say the words to yourself with me as I say them. I will always be relaxed and calm. I will not want anything to eat until dinner time.

You may substitute in place of dinner time whatever is really appropriate in the actual circumstance. It may be until lunch time, or until tomorrow, or whatever.

Now picture the spot that you looked at at the beginning of this exercise. Imagine the spot floating in, traveling together with your suggestions. Traveling all the way to the back of your head, all the way to the back. When you have your spot and your suggestions together at the back of your head, erase it, forget about the spot, forget about the suggestions, just let it all disappear. Allow yourself to relax.

Routine P

Between now and the next time I see you, you will practice this exercise faithfully at least 3 times every single day, even if you think you don't need it. It makes you feel just wonderful. And each time you go through this routine in self-hypnosis you will relax completely. You will go just as deep as you are now. Just as you are now, and the suggestions that you give yourself will go deeper and deeper into your mind. By practicing your self-hypnosis faithfully every day, you will have perfect control over your own appetite. You can dissolve away any hunger. You can dissolve away any tension, any craving for food or drink you shouldn't have. Every day your weight will keep on going down and you will keep on looking better and better, and you will keep on feeling good every single day.

Routine Q

The next time I see you, or whenever you hear my voice on tape, you will allow yourself to relax even more completely than you are now. And the suggestions I have given you will keep on going deeper and deeper and deeper into your mind.

In a few moments when you awaken yourself, you will feel very very relaxed, and you will be completely refreshed, alive, alert, full of energy, full of confidence. You will feel simply marvelous. All you have to do to awaken is to count with me from one up to five and at the count of five, open your eyes, feeling relaxed, refreshed, alert, in very high spirits. Feeling very good indeed. 1 . . 2 . . 3 . . 4 . . 5.

After the bring-out, ask the subject how she feels. Answer any questions she may have.

Have two pre-typed sheets of paper to give her to keep. These are necessary for her diet control and for practicing her self-hypnosis. One sheet has her recommended diet on it. The other sheet has her self-hypnosis routine on it. These two instruction sheets are detailed in the following two sections.

Diet Program

Breakfast:
> Small serving of protein (2-3 oz.)
> Small serving of juice or fruit (4 oz.)
> One piece of unbuttered toast

Lunch
> Small serving of protein (3-4 oz.)
> Small serving of fresh fruit or vegetable

Dinner

    Small serving of protein (4-5 oz.)

    Small salad with light dressing

    ½ cup cooked vegetable served without butter or margarine

Diet drinks, except colas, are OK.

De-caffinated coffee only.

No gravies or sauces.

Approximately 800 to 1000 calories per day.

Self-Hypnosis Instructions

Stretch! Then sit in a comfortable position.

Focus your attention on a spot, and as you do, mentally say the number 5 three times as you exhale. Then close your eyes.

Take another deep breath, and as you exhale, mentally say the number 4 three times. As you say the number 4, picture it at the same time.

Take another deep breath and do the same thing with numbers 3, 2, and 1 consecutively.

Now, imagine a relaxation force emanating from your eyes and flowing out all over your body like a warm blanket of soothing, warm, gentle air going all the way down to your toes.

Then count backward from ten to one.

After reaching the number 1, give yourself these suggestions:

    1. I will always be relaxed and calm.

    2. I will not want anything to eat until dinner.

Then picture the same spot in your mind that you looked at originally. Imagine this spot moving all the way to the back of your head taking the suggestion with it. Then forget the suggestion, so that your inner mind will absorb it.

Then count from 1 to 5 and awaken and feel the effect

of the suggestions.

Post-Session Wrap-Up

Give your client sufficient time to read the diet program and the self-hypnosis instruction sheet. Answer any questions that she may have.

You need to be fairly well informed concerning diet. It is well to have a good nutrition book on hand for reference if necessary. Many people really don't know what a protein food is, so you need to be prepared to explain and give examples.

I recommend that you read the self-hypnosis instructions out loud with your client, explaining each instruction as you go. Reaffirm that she was given these instructions under hypnosis and was given the post-hypnotic suggestion that it would work just as well for her as when you perform the hypnosis.

The most important thing the subject must understand is that she *must* practice her self-hypnosis daily. There are two reasons for this.

1. She is training her mind to follow a different course than in the past. The mind prefers to do what it has always done, i.e., follow the same path. Therefore, consistent and diligent retraining is necessary. Your mind isn't going to believe you really want to change if you take a "willy-nilly" approach to your practice of self-hypnosis. Your mind believes you really want to overeat and be fat because that is what you have been practicing and telling it for years. Now, you want to reverse that detrimental programming. To reverse it, you must hammer into your subconscious every day what you really want until your mind is convinced of your desire for a new reality; then your mind will create this new reality. . .more temperate eating habits, loss of excess weight. . .feeling better. . .looking better, etc. Fortunately, self-hypnosis doesn't take years to achieve the re-

programming.

2. Hypnotic suggestion is not permanent. If it were, it would only be necessary to have one hypnosis session and give one set of suggestions per problem and then everything would be OK. But it doesn't work that way. The length of time a hypnotic suggestion lasts effectively varies widely depending on the individual's response to hypnosis. I have seen some people who wouldn't respond to hypnotic suggestion more than a few hours to a day without the need for being reinforced with another hypnosis session. Some remain responsive for one or two weeks. A rare few, even longer than two weeks. This is why the subject needs to reinforce herself every day with the self-hypnosis until the desired results are achieved.

Case Example For Diet Control: Here is one of my case histories that applies especially to this chapter for diet control. I call it my "popcorn case".

An overweight lady came to me for diet control. Her problem was that she was a compulsive eater. She bought her popcorn in 100 pound bags. She ate it morning, noon, and night and in between times. And the popcorn was always soaked to the point of dripping with real butter and loaded with salt. Then, of course, there were cases of soda pop to drink to quench her thirst. I knew that the butter, salt, and soda pop were far more detrimental to her than the popcorn, but popcorn was the vehicle. Without the popcorn she wouldn't be consuming all those other things. So I decided to make popcorn undesirable to her.

Before hypnotizing her, I tried to find out what she didn't like. She loved everything.

"Isn't there something in life you find repulsive?" I asked in desperation.

"Well, yes. Wet chicken feathers make me ill. I can't stand the smell. My father used to make me kill and pluck chickens against my will."

There I had my mechanism. . .wet chicken feathers. When I had her into routine J and I got to the part where she puts something to eat in her mouth, I said, "There is a large bowl of popcorn in front of you. The popcorn has been soaked in wet chicken feathers. The popcorn smells like wet chicken feathers. The popcorn tastes like wet chicken feathers. Now, pick up a kernel of popcorn and put it into your mouth and taste it."

She immediately began to gag and retch. I thought she was going to vomit.

After she left my office she went home and made a batch of popcorn out of habit. This time she did vomit. She tried daily to make popcorn but got nauseous just trying to make it. By the time she came back for session 3 she had stopped trying to make popcorn. . .she had kicked the habit, and she was losing excess weight. Of course, without the popcorn, she stopped drinking soda pop and eating large amounts of butter and salt.

By session 6 she had lost around 20 pounds and was looking and feeling good. I had her add more fruit and vegetables to her diet. She was no longer a popcornaholic.

The lesson to be learned here is to find out what tastes or smells are especially offensive to your subject. Use those tastes and smells to remove the desire for the offending eating habit. Most often, the dietary habit that is causing the problem is chocolate, sweets, pastries, etc. If your subject eats five pounds of chocolate a day and she hates the taste of liver, then have her visualize getting some chocolate from the refrigerator where it has been lying next to five pounds of unwrapped wet liver. The liver taste and smell has impregnated all the chocolate. . ., etc. You get the idea.

CHAPTER 4

HYPNOSIS SESSION 3

The purpose of this session is to reinforce the hypnosis and suggestions previously given, increase the depth of hypnosis so that suggestions will be programmed in at another level of mind, and to reinforce the subject's own self-hypnosis.

The first thing that needs to be done before starting the induction is to have a dialog with the client about her experience with self-hypnosis since you last saw her. Has she been practicing her self-hypnosis faithfully every day? If not, why? Has she been following her diet faithfully? If not, why? Has she fairly well mastered the self-hypnosis or is she having some difficulties?

If she has been having difficulty with the self-hypnosis, go over the procedure with her again. Demonstrate on yourself just how to do it, speaking your thoughts out loud so she can observe and follow.

If she is having difficulty in relaxing or concentrating, reassure her that this will all disappear with practice. What she is experiencing is the same as many people first experience so do not be concerned. A frequent complaint is, "I keep forgetting what I am supposed to do in my self-hypnosis procedure." Tell her that is why you gave her the procedure written out. It is perfectly OK for her to open her eyes and read it while learning. Very quickly she will learn it from memory. Her first concern is just to learn the procedure and become comfortable with it and not be concerned about results. The results will occur automatically when she does learn and practice diligently.

Be sure to emphasize that she can change the suggestion portion of her self-hypnosis routine to suit any purpose she has in mind. She can have only one suggestion if she wants, or she can have many. I do recommend that she treat only *one* purpose or problem at any one time. Don't work on quitting smoking at the same time you are working on diet control for example. Handle them separately. The self-hypnosis routine is hers for life, so she should develop the habit of using it daily for self-enrichment of one sort or the other.

It is common at this point in the program for the subject to not be practicing her self-hypnosis regularly. This is because her recalcitrant mind is fighting change; the mind prefers to follow the same old path rather than a new one. The subject will rationalize all sorts of reasons for not being able to perform the self-hypnosis.

The two most common reasons I have been given for not practicing self-hypnosis faithfully every day are:

1. "I don't have, or cannot find, a spot to look at for beginning the self-hypnosis." Do not scold the subject for saying something this ridiculous. Remember the subject's mind is fighting her, and at the same time she is trying to understand and develop a new skill and a new lifestyle. Just calmly explain that the spot can be anything in her line of vision: a doorknob, a flower on a curtain, a dirt spot on the wall, the point in the corner where the walls and ceiling meet, an electrical outlet, an upholstery button on the sofa, a burning candle flame, an electric light bulb, and so forth. It is impossible to be in a place where there is nothing in your

line of vision on which to fix your gaze.

2. "I don't have time. I am never alone. I work in an office from 8 to 5 with people all around. Then I go home to my family where there are again demands on my time. I don't have a minute to myself." This, of course, is a common situation. It *is* often difficult to be alone for 5 minutes, 3 times a day to practice your self-hypnosis.

My response to item 2 goes something like this:

"Do you go to the toilet at all during the day?" I ask.

"Of course."

Do you take anyone with you when you go to the toilet?"

"Of course not!"

"Then every time you are sitting on the toilet, use the time to perform your self-hypnosis routine."

I didn't know it could be done sitting on the toilet," is the usual response.

"Of course you can. You can also do the self-hypnosis in the bathtub while bathing. There is no limit."

I go on to explain that self-hypnosis can be practiced anywhere, anytime successfully. In fact, when you really become good at it, you can do it with your eyes open with people and distractions all around. When you reach this point, you will really have mastered a powerful tool that you can use instantly for virtually anything. You are probably getting the impression that the potential for using your altered state of consciousness goes far beyond the scope of anything covered in this book. . .that is a correct impression. This book is just the beginning. Your mind, your thoughts have a very real potential that far transcends diet control. For now, master the things covered in this book. When you do, the next stage of your development will automatically open up to you and you will know what to do.

Occasionally you will encounter a client who is unwilling to make any good faith attempt to practice the self-hypnosis or follow the diet. This person has a vast number of reasons and counter reasons for not doing so. No matter what you say or explain, her reply is, "Yes, but. . ." When I encounter a completely non-cooperative client such as this, I say something like: "Well, if you want to pay me good money for my services and then not cooperate with those services, that certainly is your privilege. Just be aware that you will have zero results for your time and money. I do not enjoy taking money when the client is not trying to do her part. Therefore, if this continues, I will probably ask you to discontinue the sessions and save your money. Think about it. The choice is yours. Now let's proceed with today's session." I have only had to say this sort of thing twice in 12 years. Both times the clients stopped playing games and started cooperating with ultimate satisfactory results.

Now let's proceed into hypnosis session 3 which consists of 14 routines in the sequence as follows:

Session 3: A, B, C, D, E, F, I, G, H, R, L, S, T, Q

Ten of these routines have been previously given. Only routines **I, R, S, T** are new and are detailed here. Notice that the sequence is slightly different than in Session 2.

Routine I

As you breathe in, imagine that you are breathing in a pure, clean, odorless anesthesia. This anesthesia is flowing all throughout your body now, a warm, numb, tingling feeling. And the more you breathe in the more you want to breathe in, and you allow your breathing to become even deeper now, bringing in more and more of this peaceful, relaxed, tranquil feeling. From now on until the end of this session, with each breath you will allow yourself to relax more and more completely.

Routine R-1
(use only with female subjects)

As you go on floating, drifting smoothly and gently, more and more deeply relaxed with each breath, focus your attention on the tip of your nose. Keep your attention now focused gently and lazily on the tip of your nose until you reach a point where your entire attention is on the sound of my voice. When you reach that point, you can forget about the tip of your nose and just go on listening to my voice and allowing yourself to relax more and more deeply. As you keep your attention gently focused on the tip of your nose, I want you to imagine for a minute. Imagine yourself as you really want to be, slender and pretty, looking so good and feeling so fine, so full of energy and vitality, wearing the gorgeous clothes that look so good on your slender, beautiful body. This is you. This is the lovely woman you are now becoming. Every day from now on you will be more and more completely the woman you really want to be. You will be relaxed and calm no matter what is going on around you, and anything that does happen you can handle it in a relaxed and sensible manner. And you will feel so good. You will have all the energy you can use every day, and you will find it very easy to stay on your diet strictly every day, no matter where you are and no matter what you are doing.

Routine R-2
(use only with male subjects)

As you go on floating, drifting smoothly and gently, more and more deeply relaxed with each breath, focus your attention on the tip of your nose. Keep your attention now focused gently and lazily on the tip of your nose until you reach a point where your entire attention is on the sound of my voice. When you reach that point you can forget about the tip of your nose and just go on listening to my voice and allowing yourself to relax more and more deeply. As you keep your attention gently focused on the tip of your nose, I want you to imagine for a minute. Imagine yourself as you really want to be, trim and healthy, looking handsome and virile, full of confidence, energy and vitality, wearing well-fitting clothes that look so good on your proportioned, firm, trim body. This is you. This is the handsome, virile man you are now becoming. Every day from now on you will be more and more completely the man you really want to be. You will be relaxed and calm no matter what is going on around you, and anything that does happen you can handle it in a relaxed and sensible manner. And you will feel so good. You will have all the energy you can use every day, and you will find it very easy to stay on your diet strictly every day, no matter where you are and no matter what you are doing.

Routine S

You will always eat very slowly, and when you have eaten just a little bit of the proper, sensible foods you will feel full, stuffed on just a little bit of the right foods. That is all your body needs now, and that is all you will want. You will have no desire at all to nibble or snack in between meals or after dinner. You will have no desire for sweets or starches or rich greasy foods of any kind. And the longer you stay on your diet, the easier it will be. For you are now beginning to form the habit of eating correctly for your own body. And as your body responds to this habit, as your stomach keeps on shrinking a little bit every day, you will feel comfortable with less and less food, and your weight will keep on going down even faster than before. So fast, so smooth, and so easy. Every day you will keep on getting smaller and lighter and prettier, and you will feel simply marvelous every single day.

In routines where the word "prettier" is used, you may find it more appropriate to use "attractive". If the subject is a man, then use "handsome."

Routine T

You will continue to practice the self-hypnosis exercise faithfully as often as you can every single day, and each time you go through the routine in self-hypnosis you will relax completely. You will go just as deep as you are now, and whatever suggestions *you give yourself will be stronger and go deeper all the time. By continuing to practice your self-hypnosis faithfully every day, you will have perfect control over your own appetite. You can dissolve away any hunger. You can dissolve away any tension, any craving for food or drink you should not have, any fear or anger or unnecessary pain. For you are in control now, and whatever you set your mind to do, you can and will do it. You will be completely successful and you will enjoy your success. You will enjoy looking better and feeling better every single day.*

CHAPTER 5

HYPNOSIS SESSION 4

This session contains 14 hypnosis routines; 9 have been previously given and 5 are new and are detailed here. Session 4 consists of routines in the sequence as follows:

Session 4: A, B, C, D, E, F, I, G, U, V, W, X, Y, Q

This is probably the most powerful and valuable of all six hypnosis sessions covered in this book. In this session, we develop a mechanism for enabling the subject to vastly improve self-image and to deal with problems. The mechanism is the creation of a personal, private room that the subject can always go to for problem solving.

Like all sessions, you should start this session with a dialogue with the subject to find out how she is progressing with her self-hypnosis and her diet. Help her with any problems she may have encountered, then proceed with the induction.

The five new routines introduced in this session are **U, V, W, X, Y.**

Routine U

NOTE: This routine **U** is one of the most powerful and useful tools for hypnosis and self-hypnosis. At this point, we are using this routine within the context of the diet control program we are discussing. We will discuss the use of this routine further for self-hypnosis in Chapter 12. This routine creates a personal place. . .a laboratory or private temple. . .where scientific re-programming is done.

I want you to imagine now that you are standing on the top step of a heavy wooden staircase. Feel the carpet under your feet. The carpet can be any kind and color you wish. . . create it. Now extend your hand out and touch the railing. Feel the smooth polished wood of the railing under your hand. You are standing just ten steps up from the floor below. The stairs are curving very smoothly down to the floor below. In a moment we will walk down the stairs. With each step down you will allow yourself to relax even more deeply. By the time you reach the floor below you will be deeper than you have ever gone before. Take a step down now, down to the ninth step, smoothly and easily. Feel yourself going deeper. Now down to eight, deeper still. Now down to seven. . .six. . . five. . .four. . .three. . .two. . one. Now you are standing on the floor below. There is a door infront of you. Reach out and open the door. And from the room beyond the door a flood of light comes streaming out through the open doorway. Walk into the room, into the light through the open door. You are inside the room now; look around you. This is your room, and it can be anything you want it to be. Any size, any shape, any colors. You can have anything in this room that you want. You can add things, remove things, rearrange things. You can have any kind of furniture, fixtures, paintings, windows, carpets, or whatever you want because this is your place. . .your very own private inner place and you are free here. Free to create, free to be who you are. Free to do whatever you will, and the light that shines in this room is your light. Feel the light all around you, shining on the beautiful things in your room. Shining on you; feel the energy in the light. Let the light flow all through your body now. Going in through every pore in your skin. Filling you completely. Pushing away all doubt. Pushing out all fear and tension. You are filled with the light. You are clear and radiant, glowing with the shining light in your room.

Routine V-1
(use only with female subjects)

While you are standing in the light in your room, I want you to build an image. An image of yourself as you really want to be. Not as someone else wants you to be, but as you really want yourself to be. See your image standing in front of you in the light. Your image is slender, beautiful, serene and free, wearing all those gorgeous clothes that look so fine on your beautiful body. This is you. This is the real you. This is the woman you are now becoming. Walk closer to your image now. Walk closer. Now walk into the image. Let it blend into your very body. Your own best self, a living part of you now. Stronger every day.

Routine V-2
(use only with male subjects)

While you are standing in the light in your room, I want you to build an image. An image of yourself as you really want to be. Not as someone else wants you to be, but as you really want yourself to be. See your image standing in front of you in the light. Your image is trim, healthy, handsome, calm and free, wearing well-fitting clothes that look so fine on your nicely proportioned body. This is you. This is the real you. This is the man you are now becoming. Walk closer to your image now. Walk closer. Now walk into the image. Let it blend into your very body. Your own best self, a living part of you now. Stronger every day.

Routine W

From now on every day you will be more and more completely the woman you really want to be. You will be relaxed and calm. And no matter what is going on around you, you can handle it in a relaxed and sensible manner. And you will feel so good. You will have all the energy you can use every single day. And it will be so easy to stay on your diet strictly every day no matter where you are.

Routine X

You will always eat very slowly, and when you have eaten just a little bit of the proper, sensible foods you will feel full, stuffed on just a little bit of the right foods. That is all your body needs now, and that is all you will want. You will have no desire at all to nibble or snack in between meals or after dinner. You will have no desire at all for sweets or starches or rich greasy foods of any kind. All that is in the past for you now. Your body does not need that, and you do not even want it. For you are now forming the habit of eating correctly for your body. And your body is adjusting to this habit more and more completely every day. As your stomach continues to shrink a little bit every day, you will keep on going down, even faster than before, _o fast and easy. Every day you will keep on getting smaller and lighter and more attractive. And you will feel simply marvelous every day.

Routine Y

You will continue to practice your self-hypnosis exercise faithfully as often as you can every single day. And each time you go through your little routine in self-hypnosis you will relax completely. And very, very swiftly. Within just a few seconds you will go just as deep as you are now. Even deeper. And whatever suggestions you give to yourself will be stronger and deeper all the time. For you are in control now. Whatever you choose to do, you can do. Whatever you set your mind to achieve, you can and will achieve. You will be completely succesful, and you will enjoy your success. And you will enjoy becoming more and more attractive every day. You will enjoy feeling beautiful, more and more your real self every day.

CHAPTER 6

HYPNOSIS SESSIONS 5 AND 6

SESSION 5

Session 5 consists of 13 routines in the sequence as follows:

Session 5: A, B, C, D, E, F, I, G, U, W, X, Y, Q

All of these routines have already been given in previous chapters. Session 5 is nearly identical to Session 4; Session 4 had one additional routine **(V)** which is only given once to a given subject.

Session 5 is strictly a reinforcement session. This is the session I usually record on cassette tape because it is an exceptionally powerful and effective session. I give the tape to the subject to keep.

I always remind the subject that the room that she created in Session 4 and that is reinforced in Session 5 is an especially important tool for her to use. She can return to this room via her self-hypnosis anytime she wants for any good purpose she wants. In this room, she can create her own reality for a better and more enriching life. She is in direct contact with her own higher mind in this room, so she will be able to get results more effectively.

SESSION 6

Session 6 is primarily a reinforcement session consisting of 13 routines as follows:

Session 6: A, B, C, D, E, F, I, G, Z, W, X, Y, Q

Twelve of these routines have already been given in previous chapters. The one new routine, Z, is a very important one. I call routine Z the Mountain Trip. This routine allows the subject to expand her creativity and to begin to explore her own higher mind and the vast resource of higher intelligence that is available to her. I have seen some beautiful, powerful, mind-blowing experiences occur during the experiencing of this routine.

Routine Z
Mountain Trip

Find yourself lying on a soft, green meadow of grass with the bright sun overhead. Notice the flowers around your head. The gentle breeze gently blows across your body. Notice the grass and flowers spring up to about a foot above your head. See how the breeze gently blows the blades of grass back and forth. Smell the fragrance of the flowers.

Now stand up and look to the north. See the majestic mountain at the end of this meadow. Let's take a trip up that mountain. There is a stream on the right of you. Bend down and notice the cool water. Take a drink of this absolutely pure, clean, cool, refreshing water. Listen to the rush of the small rapids on this bubbly brook.

Since the stream seems to come from the mountain, let's follow it. Now we come upon a pond that is at the head of this stream. Notice how warm the water is here. Since at this level of mind we are all expert swimmers, let's go for a swim. Feel the warm sun. Feel the warm water surrounding your body as you quietly move through the water.

It is now time for us to continue up the mountain. As we climb, listen to the birds chirping. Smell the pine trees. Look at the rocks on the bank to our left. Once in a while, we can see the valley and our meadow on the right between the trees. We are halfway up the mountain now. Let's stop to rest on the rock to our right. Our meadow is in full view from here. It is now time to continue up to the top of the mountain. Listen to the squirrels chatter in the trees above.

The breeze is blowing the smell of the small cedar trees to us as we near the top. We are on the top now. We can see a deep canyon on the other side. There is a sign on the top of our mountain. It says, "Yell the questions you most want answered into the canyon below, and see the answer written in the sky above. So yell your question now. . .and see the answer in the sky above. Now ask another question. See the answer in the sky above.

Now it is time for us to return to our meadow. See the sun starting to set on the hills to the left. If we hurry, we can be off our mountain before it gets dark. Half way down the mountain now, and we stop to rest on our rock again. We can watch the beginning of the sunset. Start on down the mountain again. Hear the chirping of the small night animals. Passing our pond, we see the reflection of the sunset in its mirror surface. Our small stream is cool and refreshing as we pass along its side. Now we are back to our meadow. Lie down again in the tall grass. Smell again the flowers' fragrance. Notice the grass and flowers return to their original height as our meadow and mountain now gently fade from view.

CHAPTER 7

REGRESSION

Regression is a trip in time to an earlier period in your life. It can be an earlier period in this current life or to a past life. Hypnosis is an excellent tool for making this trip backard.

You should not attempt to regress someone until you have become a reasonably experienced hypnotist. This is because an inexperienced operator can cause it to be a traumatic and unpleasant experience for the subject. For instance, suppose you regressed a person to a past life just at the moment he or she was being beheaded; that could be a terrifying moment for your subject because it is a **real** experience. Shortly, I will detail now I traditionally perform regression and you will see how I prevent and/or handle such events in my subjects' past lives.

For certain kinds of situations, usually in the treatment of various mental or emotional disorders, it may be necessary or desirable to have the subject actually experience the pain, torment, fright or whatever. This is strictly the domain of a trained psychiatrist, psychologist, or medical doctor. If you are not in one of these three disciplines, stay 100% away from using regression in this manner.

This chapter deals with regression in a safe way for both your subject and for you.

Some hypnotists specialize in regression and do quite well. There is a lot of interest in the topic. People find it interesting and intriguing. I personally am not a regression enthusiast; it just doesn't capture my fancy very strongly. I have done enough of it to speak knowledgeably. Most of my regression work has been self-regression. Yes, it is possible to regress yourself. However, it is unlikely that you can regress yourself unless you have first been regressed by another operator and are yourself quite experienced.

This chapter is going to deal only with the technique of regressing others. I only regress persons who have been previously hypnotized either by me or someone else. I want my regression subject to be already familiar with hypnosis. This is just my personal *modus operandi;* I don't know that it is necessary. As you have probably guessed by now, I am a "play it safe" hypnotist. I do not take any chances or risks with my subjects. I recommend you do likewise. I have had to correct problems created by inept hypnotists, and it angers me that some operators are so careless and insensitive. This is part of the reason for my writing this book...to teach how hypnosis can, and should, be done in a caring, safe, helpful and professional way. People who want to learn hypnosis are going to learn it one way or the other. It is an easy skill to acquire. Hopefully, you will learn from this book to do it right.

What are the uses of regression? Here are two examples of how I used regression.

Regression Case #1: A 35 year old man came to me with chronic back pain. He had had this pain for as long as he could recall, and it was with him all of the time. Fortunately, he had an innate high tolerance for pain, but it still was a source of discomfort and irritability for him. He had no history of injury or illness. He had been to a number of physicians who all told him the same thing, "There is no physical cause for your pain." They intimated that he was imagining it. But he still felt pain; it was real.

I regressed the man back to the time when he first experienced the pain. He was 16 years old and was preparing to try out for the high school football team. The pain was so severe that he was unable to try out and never tried again. His days as an athlete were finished.

Continued investigation under hypnotic regression revealed this. He had been the football star in a small midwestern school. He was a local hero. Everyone knew him. Girls vied for his attention.

Then his father's employment caused the family to move to Chicago. He was now enrolled in a huge high school that was full of top quality athletes. Competition was fierce. His high school class alone had more students than the entire 12 grades of his previous school. Being a football hero in the small school carried no weight in this new shool.

When tryout time came, he was fearful of failure against the formidable competition. His fear was compounded because he had done considerable bragging about his previous football glories.

Guess what happened? You guessed right. He suddenly developed a severe back pain that prevented him from trying to compete. So now he had a reason that everyone would understand and sympathize with that kept him from being on the team. He now could be a knowledgeable spectator, do Monday morning quarterbacking, and revel in his past athletic achievements.

While still under hypnosis, I led him to understand the nature of his problem. Then I told him that his back pain belonged to a previous era and had no need in a later era. I told him his back pain was frozen in 1964 and that it could not leave that period. Then I slowly brought him forward in time to the present. When he opened his eyes, he was totally free of pain for the first time in his recollection. He remains free of pain today. The total time of this regression session was about one hour.

Of course, it is possible that he could create another pain (or other symptom) if he again encounters a situation that he doesn't believe he can cope with. I doubt he will though, because he learned so much from this regression about the games people can play with themselves. I also spent considerable counseling with him about how to cope and solve problems.

Regression Case #2: A 16 year old girl was my client for weight/diet control. She was a compulsive eater. The real problem was poor self-image. I had her on the six session diet control program that I've described in the earlier chapters. I saw her once a week, and my main thrust was self-image improvement. She was a superb hypnosis subject, and after just five sessions, she had lost an acceptable, healthy amount of weight, had stopped her compulsive eating, and most importantly had altered her self-image. She really liked and respected herself.

I felt that she didn't really need to return for the sixth session, and started to write her a refund check for the last session (her mother had prepaid for all six sessions).

She asked me to allow her to return for the last session. Instead of the diet program, she asked if I would do past lives regression on her for that final session. I said OK.

The regression turned out to be a beautiful experience for her, and she received two unexpected bonuses.

I took her through one death cycle and one birth cycle. She also experienced episodes in several lifetimes including the death of her husband to whom she was deeply devoted. In all of the experiences, she loved and was loved. She experienced hard work and learned the importance and satisfaction of hard work. She experienced being needed and of doing a competent job.

Here are her two bonuses:

1. She came out of the regression with an even greater feeling of self-worth and a great love of life. She developed a deep understanding in those few minutes that transformed her whole perspective about life. Everything reinforced the self-image work we had achieved in the previous five sessions.

2. And here is a real kicker: She recognized the husband who had died as being the same boy to whom she was currently engaged. They did not look the same. They had entirely different names and different nationalities. But her acute awareness under deep hypnosis brought her this knowledge.

In my regression instructions to her I had told her to go back to a previous life experience, if any, that had a direct and important relationship to her current life. What I've related here is the result. Regression can be a beautiful, powerful, and beneficial experience when properly done.

Getting Ready: We have just taken a big picture look at regression along with an example of a current life regression and a past life regression. Now let's see how it is done.

First, you use a series of deep relaxation and visualization techniques to achieve hypnosis exactly as detailed in the earlier chapters. The specific routines and sequence are your choice based on your own experience and preference. For our purposes here use the routines as follows:

A, B, C, D, E, F, I, G, H

When you finish directing routine **H**, you start into the regression routine which is detailed in the next paragraph. The regression routine I give is a general approach. You will have to improvise your own wording right on the spot to fit your needs. To direct a person to a current life regression you use different words than to direct to a past life regression. When you question the subject under hypnosis and carry on a dialogue, you will need to question or say whatever is appropriate. In large measure, what you ask or direct are dependent on the answers you receive from the subject.

Regression Routine:

Now I am going to count backward from 10 to 1. Each number I say will take you to an even deeper state of relaxation. When I reach 1, you will find yourself standing on a white sand beach facing a beautiful, deep blue ocean. 10 - 9 - 8 - 7 - 6 - 5 - 4 - 3 - 2 - 1. You are now standing on a white sand beach facing a beautiful, deep blue ocean. The ocean is the ocean of life, and it stretches endlessly before you, and to the left, and to the right. You are standing on the sands of time. The sands of time stretch endlessly to your left and to your right. Now turn your head and look to your left. The sands of time are stretching endlessly into the future. Notice a fog bank on the beach that prevents you from currently seeing beyond it. Now turn your head and look to your right. The sands of time are stretching endlessly into the past. Notice a fog bank on the beach that prevents you from currently seeing beyond it.

In a few moments, we are going to walk down the beach to the right, into the fog bank that is currently clouding the past. You will always be able to hear my voice and follow my instructions. When I ask you questions you will be able to answer me verbally out loud.

Now I want you to turn to your right and walk down the sands of time into the past. Into the fog bank. The fog bank now surrounds you competely. It is cool, refreshing, and comfortable. You may stop walking now. Just stand in the fog bank. In a few moments, I will count backward from 10 to 1, and each number I say will take you further and further back in time as the fog bank begins to dissolve. When I reach 1, the fog bank will be completely dissolved and you will find yourself in a previous life experience, if there were any, that had a direct and important relationship to your current life. Any experiences you may have you will view as though you are watching a movie. You will have complete awareness of all detail, of your thoughts and emotions, of who you are, where you are, what you are doing. Just as in a movie, you will be aware of joy or pain, sorrow or love, awareness of all feeling and emotion, but you will not physically experience it. You will be able to observe it and tell me about it. Anytime I say the word "RELAX", whatever experience you are having at the time will immediately disappear, and you will take a deep breath and settle into peaceful relaxation while listening to the sound of my voice and following my directions.

I am now going to count from 10 down to 1, and you will go progressively back in time with each count down. At the count of 1, the fog bank will be entirely dissolved and you will find yourself in a previous life experience.

10 - 9 - 8 - 7 - 6 - 5 - 4 - 3 - 2 - 1. You are now in a previous life experience. Look around you. What do you see? (Wait for response) Who are you? (Wait for response).

Note: At this point your dialog must be improvised. If the subject should encounter an experience that is undesirable and causes anxiety, just say "RELAX". The experience will disappear, and you can direct her to another experience by the following: I am now going to count from 1 to 3 and snap my fingers. At that time you will find yourself (here fill in your own words for whatever is appropriate such as "in another past life experience", or "one year later", or "a day earlier", etc.) 1 - 2 - 3 (snap fingers). You are now (again fill in your own words for whatever is appropriate).

When you are ready to bring the subject back to the current time and awaken her, say the following: Relax and go deeper. In a few moments I am going to count from 1 up to 10. When I reach 10 you will be back to (here say the current time, date, and year; for example, 5 pm, July 4, 1986) *and you will be aware of sitting comfortably in a chair with your eyes still closed. 1 - 2 - 3 - 4 - 5 - 6 - 7 - 8 - 9 - 10. It is now* (repeat the time, date, and year) *and you are relaxing comfortably in a chair with your eyes still closed. I am now going to count from 1 to 5 and snap my fingers. At that time you will open your eyes and be wide awake and feeling fine. You will have complete recall of everything you have just experienced. 1 - 2 - you are coming up slowly now - 3 - at the count of five you will open your eyes and be wide awake and feeling fine - 4 - 5* (snap fingers). *Open eyes! Wide awake and feeling fine!*

Analysis: Discuss as much or as little concerning the regression session with your subject as either of you care to. The discussion provides a great learning tool for both of you.

The wording in the regression procedure is very important. Do not be tempted to take short cuts. Notice the symbology and visualization I use in the beginning...sands of time...ocean of life...fog bank, etc. Notice I said "we are going to walk down the beach...I didn't say "you". This is because I want the subject to know she is not alone on this trip; it keeps me in her acute awareness no matter where she goes. That way I am always present to help her and converse with her.

Notice I emphasize that she will always be able to hear my voice and follow my instructions and converse with me. I am her security blanket, so to speak.

Notice how I handled the situation so she will not feel trauma, but will still be aware of it by employing the movie screen as a mechanism. Notice I built in the key word "RELAX" as a device to leave an experience. This is both a safety tool and a transition tool.

To go deeper, I count down. For coming out, I count up. Notice that I first tell the subject what I am going to do..."In a moment I will count, etc. and you will be aware, etc." Then I say, "I am now going to count, etc. and you are aware, etc." A subtle, but important change of wording.

I tell the subject that she will have total recall when she awakens. Strictly speaking, this is not necessary because the subject always has recall after hypnosis unless the operator tells her that she won't. I feel recall is the whole advantage of regression, so I throw that statement in just as a reinforcement. It is like putting clear plastic tape over the stamp on an important letter after you have already glued it on the envelope. . .just to make sure. Leave that sentence out of the procedure if you wish.

Regression requires quite a bit of preparation on the part of the operator. You need to think through the purpose of the regression in advance. Have the general direction of your questions clearly in mind. And be prepared to improvise on the spot for whatever direction the events take.

Do not put words in the subject's mouth, or suggest to the subject what she might expect to experience. Notice that in the procedure I do not say she WILL go to a past life experience. I say, ". . .previous life experience, IF THERE WERE ANY. . ."

Under hypnosis, the subject will always try to please the operator. If you say to a man, "Go to a previous life experience where you were a woman," he will create such a life if there really wasn't one. When he creates it, he will be aware that he is making it up, but he doesn't care because that is what you asked for.

Choose your words very carefully or you will likely not have a valid regression session. Do not impose your own ideas or concepts on the subject.

One final note about excursions in time. In my procedure, I said the future is to the left, and it is. So is it possible to progress in time as well as regress? Yes, it is. I am not covering this subject in this book. You probably should not fool around with progression until you are very, very experienced in all other phases of hypnosis. However, the mechanism is there to do so.

There are many, many other regression techniques that work fine. This is mine. Use it, or develop your own, or use some other one that you may run across in talking with other hypnotists.

CHAPTER 8

SUGGESTIONS

This chapter contains a collection of suggestions that could be appropriate to give for a variety of purposes. The suggestions given here are grouped by the type of problem being handled. This list of suggestions certainly isn't all inclusive. The intent is to provide you with a start upon which you can enlarge or modify for your specific needs.

Auras
Your aura radiates from you with the strength and colors that you decide by your mental, physical and emotional condition. You choose to be in such a positive, healthy, balanced state that your aura is powerful, clear and brilliant with the beneficial energy you desire.

You can visualize your aura as you wish it to be, and then command your higher self with these words: "I am now becoming the kind of person I need to be to radiate the aura I visualize and desire."

Concentration & Memory
You will feel a tremendous and intense concentration power with everything you do, and you will remember more effectively everything you concentrate on.

Your mind will be like a soft, absorbent sponge and everything you concentrate on you will absorb like a sponge. When you want to remember that which you have concentrated on, you will squeeze your mind like a sponge and you will remember everything you have concentrated on.

You will feel a tremendous amount of energy with a tremendous concentration power.

You will feel a tremendous drive and concentration power with everything you do.

You have an excellent mind, and you will use it more effectively from now on every day.

Depression

To help prevent depression or to overcome it if you are in it, you can say and think these words: "Positive thoughts bring me benefits and advantages I desire." You will direct and allow your mind to drift to positive, happy, constructive thoughts.

You will not allow anyone or anything to determine how you are going to feel. You are in control, and you choose to feel happy, important, and worthy.

You are the most important person in your world, and you will not allow anyone or anything take that dignity away from you.

You are a fighter, and you fight for your birthright to be happy and in balance with your entire being.

Drinking

Since you will feel relaxed, your fingers will be relaxed, and you will not reach for alcohol to drink.

You have made a decision to not drink alcohol. You will feel free of the desire to drink alcohol, and you will not drink it.

You will feel the strength to stay away from alcohol, and you will stay away from alcohol.

Group Confidence

When you see people, you will feel very talkative and very

happy, and you will talk and you will smile.

You will push yourself to go out and mix socially with people. You will feel very at ease in the presence of people.

You will push yourself to meet people. You will take the initiative. You will feel the drive to go out and meet people, and you will start the conversation with ease.

You will feel the energy, drive, and desire to go out socially, and you will go out socially.

You will feel positive that everything in life will work out for you, and you will feel good about it.

You will feel confident that you are just as intelligent as anyone else and even more so. You will realize that you can talk and think just as intelligently as anyone else, and you will feel confident in all situations.

Healing

When you are injured, all you need to do to relieve the pain and promote healing is to place either hand on the injured area and say or think the word gone while visualizing the area to be normal and healthy, while healing energy from your hand penetrates the area.

You can promote healing in any area of your body by visualizing that area to be flooded in healing white light, and visualizing the area to be normal and healthy.

You can help maintain and promote good health by saying and thinking these words every day: "Every day in every way I am getting better, better, and better."

When confronted with a possible illness, you can rally your body's natural powers to defeat the illness by slowly scanning your body with your visual intelligence from head to toe, pausing briefly at each portion of your body to visualize health, normality and perfection. If your intelligence detects an abnormality, you can immediately correct it to be normal in your mind. Your body's function and balance will follow the directions you visualize and command in your mind.

Language Study
(Insert language desired)
When you study Spanish, you will intensely concentrate as you study, and you will remember all the Spanish you have concentrated on.

When you attempt to speak Spanish, all the Spanish you have studied will come to you easily and quickly, and you will speak Spanish with great ease and confidence.

You will feel a tremendous desire to learn the Spanish language, and as you study this language you will feel a tremendous concentration power, and you will remember everything you concentrate on.

Longevity
You desire a long, healthy, happy life, and your mind will direct your activities and thought patterns so you will realize this goal.

You are what you think. You are now commanding your mind to always direct you to lead your life in such a manner as to promote a long, healthy, happy life. And you will listen to and follow the beneficial dictates of your mind.

Love & Trust
You will take people as they are. You will radiate warmth, and you will see people radiate it back.

You will feel the natural freedom to love mentally, and you will feel free of fear and free of rejection.

You will not categorize or stereotype people as being like other people you have experienced, because you will realize inherently that they are not like other people.

Miscellaneous
When speaking in front of a group of people, you will intense-

ly concentrate on your speech and you will remember easily the entire subject matter of your speech. You will speak with confidence and be free of self-consciousness.

You will speak out easily on everything you want to say in front of one person or in front of a group of people.

When you are performing in front of people, you will feel that you are performing just as well or even better than anyone else performing. You will feel free of the thought that people are just watching you. You will feel relaxed regardless of who watches.

When talking to people or in front of a group of people, you will feel a tremendous and powerful concentration power. You will remember everything with ease, and you will talk with ease. Your throat and chest will be relaxed, and you will feel free of all dryness and choking sensations.

When you speak publicly, you will feel relaxed and confident that you will sound very natural and very intelligible. You will speak with great ease.

You will feel very relaxed and yet very alert.

Every day in every way you will feel better, better, and better.

Positive thoughts bring you benefits and advantages you desire.

You are in control.

Money Management

You are now making a commitment to yourself to budget your money wisely by not every allowing yourself to spend or commit to spend money you do not actually have in your possession.

You are now resolving to completely eliminate impulsive buying. You will go shopping only when you need specific items which you have listed on a paper, and you will not allow yourself to purchase any item that was not originally on your list, no matter what.

The words **BARGAIN** and **SALE** no longer entice you. You realize those words are used by someone else to get your money.

You purchase only what you truly need, and you do not allow merchants to decide what you need or want.

Physical Exercise

You will have the desire to physically exercise. You will find time each day to physically exercise, and you will exercise your body vigorously. And when you have done this, you will feel simply great.

Phobias
(Insert phobia)

You will feel relaxed and at ease in an airplane. You will feel relaxed, confident, and free of fear, and you will be free of fear.

Procrastination

You will not put off doing the things you have to do. You will organize the things you have to do, and you will do them and get them out of the way.

Reading & Study

You will read faster and comprehend easier everything you read.

You will look forward to going to school, and you will have a serious interest in all the courses you take.

You will feel a desire to study your courses. You will concentrate tremendously on your study, and you will remember everything you concentrate on.

You will feel confident that when you take the (insert the name) exam, you will be relaxed. You will easily remember the answers you already know without tension. Right before and during the exam you will feel relaxd and confident and everything will come to you.

Time Management

You are now making a commitment to yourself to not put off

until tomorrow what can and should be done today.

You will become consciously aware everytime you want to procrastinate, and you will immediately resolve not to procrastinate. You will immediately do what needs to be done.

You are becoming more conscious of time and of what you can realistically achieve in any period of time. This enables you to plan more effectively, and to execute those plans more efficiently. You are becoming a better and better planner every day.

Self-Confidence
You will think of the present and future only.

It will be so easy for you to achieve the success and happiness you want and deserve. For you are the product of your own thought patterns. Think success, and you are a success. Think beauty, and you are beautiful. Think strength, and you are strong. Think positively and constructively, and your life becomes a positive and constructive experience. These things are your new image. . .the new you. . . stronger and stronger every day.

You are now learning to be in total control of every aspect of your life. You will always be relaxed and calm and in control. No longer will you allow others to exercise control over you. You are in control.

You are a beautiful, intelligent, and worthwhile person. And every day from now on you will become more completely the person you really want to be. You will be confident, relaxed, poised, charming, optimistic, and firm in your resolution to do what you want for your own happiness.

Never again will you be a slave to anything, to any person, or to any job. You are your own person, and you are in total control.

Sex, Female Subject
When you have sexual relations, you will feel relaxed and you will reach a climax.

You will feel a natural physical attraction toward the oppo-

site sex.

When you have sexual relations, you will not block. You will not fear failure. You will feel positive and confident that you will have an orgasm, and you will naturally have an orgasm.

When you have sexual relations with a man, you will feel tremendous physical desire for him. When you feel him penetrate your body, you will experience heightened excitement and enjoyment and will have multiple orgasms during the entire lovemaking period.

NOTE: The following two suggestions are especially helpful for frigidity.

You will always find that the touch and sight of your male companion is exciting and sexually stimulating. Even the slightest physical contact with your love companion will cause you to desire sexual relations, and you will reach a climax and have multiple orgasms.

Every day your sexual appetite will be stronger and stronger, and you will feel better and better. You will find yourself becoming more and more sexually responsive to your love partner by easily becoming aroused and experiencing orgasms.

Sex, Male Subject

When you have sexual relations, you will feel relaxed and you will achieve erection and ejaculation.

You will feel a natural physical attraction toward the opposite sex.

When you have sexual relations, you will not block. You will not fear failure. You will feel positive and confident that you will have a firm, lasting erection and have a satisfying ejaculation.

Whenever you have sexual relations with a woman, you will have a powerful ejaculation and a complete release of semen from the seminal vessels.

When you have sexual relations with a woman, you will feel a tremendous physical desire for her. When you penetrate this *woman you will have a very stiff, rigid erection. You will maintain this erection until the woman has climaxed, and only then will you have an ejaculation.*

When you have physical relations with a woman, you will have a very stiff, rigid erection. You will feel great pleasure, and it will feel good.

NOTE: The following two suggestions are especially helpful for impotence.

You will always find that the touch and sight of a female companion is sexually stimulating. Even the slightest physical contact with a consenting woman will cause you to desire sexual relations, and your penis will become firm and erect.

Every day your sexual appetite will be stronger and stronger, and you will feel better and better. You will find yourself becoming more and more sexually responsive to your love partner by easily getting and maintaining a rigid erection.

Sleep
When you go to sleep this evening, you will quickly drop off into a deep, sound sleep for 8 hours. The next thing you know, it will be daylight, and you will awaken refreshed and alert.

Smoking
Regardless of what happens at work, you will feel relaxed. You will feel free of the desire to smoke the entire working time.

You are in total control of every aspect of your life. Cigarettes no longer have any part in your life. You are now a non-smoker. You will remain a non-smoker the rest of your life. You have made this healthy decision, and you are happy with that decision. You are in control. Cigarettes have no control over you any longer. You have resolved to break the bad habit of smoking, and you have broken that bad habit.

Weight
You will feel satisfied with very small quantities of food, and

these small quantities of food will satisfy you completely.

You will feel the strength to stay away from, and you will stay away from, sweets, starches, flour, etc.

You will have no desire to eat anything between meals or after dinner at night. After dinner, you will have no desire to eat anything until breakfast tomorrow morning.

All the calories in the foods you eat will be completely utilized by your body and not stored as unnecessary fat.

You will strictly follow the diet you prescribe for yourself, eating nothing between meals or after dinner. You will eat only the foods prescribed by your diet, and when you have done this you will no longer feel hungry.

Work Success

You will handle all situations on the job in a very relaxed, calm, and sensible manner, free of tension.

During your working hours you will feel relaxed and calm. Regardless of what happens, you will handle every situation in a relaxed, calm, and sensible manner, free of tension.

You will make decisions on the job, and you will feel great confidence in your decisions.

In your working hours on the job, you will feel a powerful and intense concentration power on your work. You will work very, very fast with a tremendous amount of energy.

You will look forward to the job interview. You will feel completely at ease during job interviews. You will feel confident that you will radiate all the personable and knowledgeable qualities and work interest that the employer seeks. You will speak in a calm, concise, and meaningful manner without tension.

You will feel an intense interest in your work, and you will feel a tremendous drive to perform to the best of your ability.

You are a successful person, and you enjoy your success. Part of your success is your ability to manage your time efficiently. You plan your time and your projects, and you execute your plan promptly without allowing yourself to be distracted.

You will provide honest and sincere service for your customers, knowing that your rewards will follow as a result.

You are capable and efficient, and your creative mind knows what you can do. Your creative mind will find a way to lead you into the right circumstances and situations to best take advantage of your abilities.

You are learning to relax. . .to release all anxiety and relax and let go. For you are in control of all aspects of your life now. No longer will you allow anxiety, tension, or nervous energy to impede you. Every day you will notice yourself relaxing more. You will notice yourself becoming more calm and more in control than every before.

You will notice every day that your attitude is becoming more and more philosophical and free of serious concern about life's daily problems.

You are an excellent salesman, and each day you will feel yourself becoming even more successful as the new, confident, relaxed YOU becomes more and more prominent in your personality.

CHAPTER 9

POTPOURRI

This chapter contains a collection of important material that doesn't fit neatly into the other chapters of the book.

Hypnosis For Children
The techniques and routines covered thus far in this book are for adults, specifically for about ages 15 and up.

Children don't need such lengthy procedures because their brain activity is already predominently in alpha. It is much easier and faster to induce hypnosis in children; the younger they are, the faster they respond and the shorter the procedure needed. Also, their attention span is such that they won't listen to a lot of boring words. Hypnosis for children often makes use of physical contact. Shortly, I will give one case history and several fast routines.

I also use these quick children's routines quite effectively on adults whom I have previously hypnotized and on those who have a very short attention span due to some sort of infirmity. Quick routines are also excellent for relieving pain or anxiety in an emergency situation.

Case History: Mary (not her real name), age 11, had been experiencing constant earache in her left ear for many days due to a severe infection. Her physician had given her medication for the infection, but it was working very slowly. The pain relievers just were not working at all.

I had her stand in front of me with her left ear facing me.

I asked, "What is your problem?"

She replied tearfully, "My ear hurts."

"Do you want it to hurt?"

"No."

"Would you like me to take away the pain?"

She nodded yes.

"Close your eyes, Mary. I am putting my hand by your ear about a quarter inch away. Do you feel the warmth of my hand?" (I had the palm of my right hand covering her left ear, not touching it, about one quarter inch away).

"Yes."

"Good. Now I want you to imagine that you have an eye inside you that can go anywhere inside your body and look at things. Can you do that?"

"Yes."

"Good. Now look inside your left ear with that eye where you feel the warmth of my hand. Can you see the inside of your ear?"

"Yes."

"Very good. Now imagine strong energy coming from my hand into your ear. This energy will help you. Now I want you to light up the inside of your ear with your own energy. It will be like turning on a light in a dark cave. Light up your ear with the energy. This is your healing energy which takes away all pain and causes the ear to get well. Have you done this?"

"Yes." She is smiling now.

"Mary, I am going to count from 1 to 3 and snap my fingers. When I do, you will open your eyes and your ear will feel fine, and it will continue to feel fine. 1 - 2 - 3. (snap).

Open eyes and feeling fine."

She opened her eyes and smiled. "Thank you," she said.

The pain was gone and she ran off to play.

This entire procedure probably lasted two minutes. I merely directed the child's tremendous creative ability to bring about results.

By the way, the infection rapidly cleared up and was gone in another 24 hours.

There are several important points I want you to make strong mental note of concerning my technique in this case. I asked Mary what was wrong. I knew what was wrong, but it is important for her to define the problem and thus focus her attention on it. I asked if she wanted the problem. Again, I knew the answer, but by her saying, "No", she is making a commitment to herself to get rid of the problem. Then I asked if she wants my help. Her "Yes" answer solidifies her commitment and puts her faith in me and in what I am going to do. At this point, the problem is already half solved. From that point on, I just utilize and direct her own creative energies to solve the rest of the problem.

Children's minds are very powerful because they don't clutter up their beliefs with all of the artificial and false nonsense that most adults do.

Children have not yet acquired the inhibitions and artificial barriers in their thinking and behavior that most adults have. As a result, children respond to hypnotic suggestions easily, quickly, and very effectively. It takes longer to condition adults—to bypass their inhibitions—to reach the child within them. Children think, "I can!" Most adults tend to think, "I can't!" As the Roman poet Virgil wrote over 2000 years ago, "They can because they think they can!"

Children's Routine #1: This routine is especially effective for ages 5 to 8 years old. These children's brain activity is almost exclusively in alpha, so hypnosis and suggestion are very quickly effective. The induction procedure is almost entirely a physical, rather than verbal, procedure. The suggestions are brief and to the point. Typically this entire procedure won't be more than about 2 minutes long, and can be used for most any purpose from bed wetting to fear of the dark.

Have the child stand straight against a wall with feet together and heels against the wall. Place a chair for yourself about 2 feet in front of the child and sit in it. Instruct the child as follows:

Tommy, when I tell you, I want you to start bending over. You will soon lose your balance and start to fall forward, and I will catch you. At this point, extend your arms and keep them extended to show the child you can and will catch him.

When you feel yourself fall into my arms, just close your eyes and rest in my arms while I talk to you for just a short time. Do you understand? If he doesn't understand, explain until he does, then proceed.

All right, Tommy, start to bend over now. Keep bending until you fall into my arms.

When he falls into your arms say, *Close your eyes and just rest here in my arms for a short time while I talk to you.*

At this point you say your suggestions. For example:

Tiny babies wet the bed because they are so small they are not able to go to the bathroom. Big people do not wet the bed because they know how to go to the bathroom any time they want to. You are a big person, Tommy, and you get bigger every day. You know how to go to the bathroom whenever you need to go. Even if you are sleeping in bed, you will wake up if you need to go to the bathroom, and you will get up and go to the bathroom as soon as you wake up. You will not wet the bed any more because you now know how to wake up and go to the bathroom by yourself. You will feel good every time you get up and go to the bathroom instead of wetting the bed.

I am now going to stand you up, and you can open your eyes and be wide awake. Gently stand the child upright and say, *Open eyes! Wide awake and feeling fine!*

It is not unusual for the child to ask to go to the bathroom immediately upon awakening from this brief hypnosis session. When he does, it immediately reinforces the suggestion.

Here is a brief analysis of the salient points of this procedure:

1. Every child knows he can easily bend over without losing his balance. Yet when you tell him to bend, he does lose his balance and falls into your arms just as you said he would. This immediately establishes his confidence and trust in you because it happened just as you said it would even though he doesn't know why. The reason why (which you do **not** explain) is that it is impossible for anyone to stand flush against a wall with feet together and then bend over without falling. This is because the buttocks push against the wall when you bend, thrusting the body forward and off balance. This is why the procedure is good for younger children but not for older ones who could easily figure it out.

2. You hold the child in your arms. This establishes contact and rapport. Also, the child is in a physical position that keeps him from fidgeting or engaging in any sort of physical distraction.

3. Your suggestion is brief, logical, and to the point. It should always be a positive suggestion that makes the child feel good about himself. Notice in the example, I capitalize on every child's desire to be big and to achieve goals that big people achieve.

4. The wake up is simple and quick. He knows when you have assisted him to his feet and let go that it is all over, and he is in charge again.

Children's Routine #2: This routine is excellent for all ages from 5 to 100. I especially like it for children from about 9 to 14. This procedure also utilizes some physical positioning and physical contact with a minimum of verbal speaking. The entire procedure will last about 5 to 7 minutes, depending on the extent of your suggestions.

Seat the child in a straight-back, armless chair positioned so no harsh light falls on her eyes. Have her rest her arms in her lap. Feet flat on the floor and slightly apart.

You stand immediately in front of her, slightly to her right. A good way to position yourself is to have your right foot between her two feet, but not touching. This puts your right eye in approximately the same vertical plane as her right eye.

Have her gaze straight ahead. This brings her line of vision about at your waist or chest, depending on your height and hers.

Put the tip of your right index finger on your own right cheekbone just under your right eye and say, *Karen, I want you to keep your head facing straight ahead. Just roll your eyes upward to focus your gaze on my right finger which I am holding beneath my right eye.*

In a moment I am going to slowly move my finger from my cheek, through the air, and touch your forehead. I want you to follow the movement of my finger with your eyes until I touch your forehead. When you feel my finger touch your forehead, I want you to close your eyes, take a deep breath, and relax. Now watch my finger.

Start moving your finger slowly from your cheek, through the air toward her forehead. Take 5 to 10 seconds to do this to allow her plenty of eye concentration and strain.

When you touch her forehead say, *Eyes closed! Take a deep breath, and relax.* Remove your finger from her forehead.

Allow your head to droop slightly as all your neck muscles relax. Feel this relaxation flow up into your face and eyes, a warm tingling feeling. Allow this relaxation to flow downward throughout your entire body now. Feel the warm, tingling relaxation go into your shoulders, your chest, waist, hips, thighs, calves, ankles, feet and toes. Completely relaxed from head to toes.

In a moment, I am going to gently pick up each of your hands, one at a time, and let them drop back onto your lap. Each time I do, you will relax even more completely.

Using your right thumb and forefinger, gently grasp her right wrist and raise her hand about 2 inches from her lap, then release your grip allowing the hand to flop back onto her lap. Say *Relax* at the moment you drop the hand. Do this three times with her right hand, and then do it three times with her left hand.

At this point you give the suggestions. For example:

I want you to imagine now that you are in school at your desk taking your spelling exam. You are relaxed and confident. You are intelligent and you have a perfect memory. You can easily remember anything you have studied. See your teacher standing in front of the class. She pronounces the first spelling word. You quickly write the word on your paper. You have spelled it correctly. The teacher pronounces word after word after word, and you easily write them all down correctly. It feels so good to you. You notice that some other children seem to be having problems, but you do not have a problem because you have learned to relax and let your excellent mind easily do the work for you. And tomorrow when you take your spelling exam, you will be just as relaxed as you are now and your mind will work easily and correctly to furnish you all the information you need to spell all the words correctly. You are a bright, capable person in everything you put your mind to do.

Now I am going to count from 1 to 3 and snap my fingers. When I snap my fingers you will open your eyes, be wide awake, feeling fine and full of mental energy and confidence. 1 - 2 - 3. (Snap) Open eyes! Wide awake and full of energy and confidence.

Here is a brief analysis of the salient points of this procedure:

1. The physical positioning is very important. You stand in front of her so she must look up to you. This puts you in an authoritative position in her eyes so she will automatically follow your direction without question. However, you stand slightly to one side so as not to completely block her. This keeps her from becoming intimidated or apprehensive.

2. The finger to forehead movement causes her eyes to roll upward and become slightly tired or strained. This action automatically triggers the alpha level of brain activity.

3. You use a quick physical relaxation procedure which is reinforced and deepened by the hand dropping routine.

4. This procedure is somewhere in between the young children's procedure and the full adult procedure. It is a very effective procedure for all ages. I use it frequently.

Summary: Hypnosis procedures for children are short and fast. Usually the procedures involve a liberal use of physical activity or contact to implement the induction. The suggestions need to be carefully structured to get the message across completely and quickly in an upbeat manner. The two procedures I've detailed here are two I use often, but by no means are these the only ones. These examples provide you with a good start.

I do very little, if any, pre-hypnosis counseling with children because they don't need it. Their minds are not cluttered with erroneous pre-conceived ideas like most adults' minds are.

Children accept things as they are, and respond accordingly. In many ways, they are more adult than adults, so I treat them that way. This brings up my one ironclad rule in dealing with children: Never talk down to them or treat them in a condescending manner. They are every bit my equal and deserve to be treated respectfully and equally.

Group Hypnosis

There will be times when you are a speaker to a high school or college class, a club or other organization, or even an informal house party. You can make the highlight of your presentation a brief deep-relaxation session for the entire group. You use the same routines as you would for an individual. Since you are not interested in solving specific problems, you just use a few routines that will give a light hypnosis. Put in a few generic suggestions, and then bring them out.

Pre-Hypnosis Instructions: Before you get into the demonstration, you should have given a speech about hypnosis. In addition to this, I have two rules:

1. There is to be no smoking in the room prior to the start of the lecture or during the lecture and demonstration. (I also do not allow smoking in the room where I do individual hypnosis sessions). In other words, there must be no presence of smoke . . . not even residual smoke. The reason is that in the altered state of consciousness people become hypersensitive, and smoke, even from one cigarette, can trigger coughing in some people.

2. I instruct the group that if they choose to not participate, that is fine. They can just sit with their eyes open and watch, or leave the room if they wish. I only ask that they do not disturb those who are participating. I also tell those who do participate that if they want to, they can open their eyes and take a peek at what is going on. I stress that this is just a mini-demonstration of deep relaxation techniques. Knowing that they can choose, that they can peek, etc. makes them more comfortable and allays any apprehen-

sions they may have. I have never yet had anyone who wouldn't participate or who opened their eyes to peek.

The Demonstration Routine: Give routines **A, B, C, F, G, I** (or whatever other arrangement you prefer). Then give some generic suggestions such as:

1. You are now in a very healthy, relaxed state and you can use this state to achieve any worthwhile goal.

2. You are a good, worthy person and every day you will learn more about using your mind and skills in a beneficial way.

3. You are a successful person and you enjoy your success.

4. I will stop talking now for 30 seconds to give you time to program your own individual goal. (Then stop talking and time the 30 seconds on your watch).

When the 30 seconds are up, bring them out using a routine similar to routine **Q.**

Close with a question and answer dialogue about the experience. You can usually get this going by asking, "Tell me about your experience." If there is reluctance to speak first, pick out someone and say, "How about you, Diane. Did you relax? Did you have a goal that you programmed?", etc.

Stage Hypnosis

The stage hypnotist is a performer who is also a very good hypnotist. His purpose is to entertain, and he does so by selecting subjects from the audience who are good hypnosis subjects and then has those subjects perform funny or incredible acts while under light hypnosis.

In the beginning he doesn't know who in the audience is a good subject, but he knows that statistically there are three or four in any group of a dozen he could pick. So he invites a dozen volunteers onto the stage. People who volunteer for this sort of thing tend to be uninhibited and free wheeling; the hypnotist knows this and this is what he wants.

He uses a few quick routines on his dozen volunteers and observes them carefully. He really knows people and his trade. It is easy for him to spot those who will give him problems; he either asks these to return into the audience, or else he leaves them on stage but doesn't use them.

Then moving quickly, he concentrates on the ones he knows are likely to respond well. He uses quick routines to induce light hypnosis. He then directs the subjects to perform entertaining acts. For example, he might get a man to give a stirring speech on behalf of women's liberation, or get a subject to bark like a dog. The repertoire can be nearly limitless.

In the stage demonstrations I have seen, the hypnotist has always told his subjects, "When you awaken you will not remembe anything that happened while you were hypnotized." Since a hypnotized person always remembers unless he is told he won't, I suppose the stage hypnotist does this so the subject won't feel embarrassed afterwards.

The several stage hypnotists I have seen were quite skilled. They were sensitive to their subjects, and used methods that were safe.

However, a clumsy or careless hypnotist could potentially do harm to his subjects.

I have not done stage hypnosis and do not intend to. I have no interest in it. To me, hypnosis is a valuable tool for helping people enrich their lives. A good stage hypnotist is somewhat like a great brain surgeon who restricts his practice to removing skin warts. There is nothing wrong with it, but what a waste of skill.

I suspect some stage hypnotists earn their living that way, and use their skills off stage to help people.

CHAPTER 10

ADDITIONAL CASE HISTORIES

Throughout the book I have included case histories to illustrate certain points and techniques. Included in this chapter are a few more brief profiles of other cases to give you an even broader perspective of the uses of hypnosis. I have tried to pick some of the more interesting cases. I haven't even scratched the surface as far as illustrating all of the kinds of cases I've had, but I think within the covers of this book there are sufficient examples to give you the idea of what you may encounter and how you might want to handle it.

Here are some of the types of cases I've handled using hypnosis over the years:

diet control
various phobias and fears, for
   example:
    fear of death
    fear of failure
    fear of inadequacy
memory improvement
impotency
aches and pains-such as migraines
sexual problems
insomnia

smoking
guilt for various reasons, for
    example:
    abortion
regression
test taking
suicidal
habit control-stress control
self-image improvement
skill enhancement
lack of energy

Test Taking Case: When my youngest daughter, Eileen, was 15 she was taking a typing course in high school. In order to get an A in the course for the semester, she had to type 45 words per minute. She could type even faster than that when not under pressure, but she froze up on tests. The very word "test" caused her brain and fingers to go out to lunch.

The night before her big test, I hypnotized her. Under hypnosis I had her visualize herself typing at lightning speeds with no errors, all the while feeling calm, at ease, and in total control. Then I gave her the post hypnotic suggestion that she would type 45 words per minute the next day on her typing test, and that she would remain relaxed throughout the entire test.

She typed exactly 45 words per minute on the test which earned her an A. She reported feeling so relaxed and confident throughout the test.

Notice here that hypnosis did not enable Eileen to do something she wasn't normally capable of. She had the capability, but had been putting obstacles in her path. Hypnosis removed those obstacles, allowing her to express her ability. She typed exactly 45 words per minute bcause that is what I had told her to do under hypnosis. If I had said 50 words, she would have done that because that was still in her ability range. If I had said 200 words per minute, she would not have done it because that was beyond her ability, but she would have certainly tried to do it. I don't know what the outcome would have been if I had said 200 words a minute. My guess is that the effort and resulting failure could have introduced another problem and frustration. So, be careful of what to suggest to your subjects. You want to enable them and improve them, not introduce additional problems.

Insomnia Case: An elderly lady came in for a free consultation to see what my fees were and if I could help her overcome her insomnia. Typically, she lay awake nearly all night, every night, not getting her needed rest. She was on social security and couldn't afford a multi-session program. She felt all she could afford was one $25 session.

"Couldn't you help me in just one session?" she pleaded.

I have a special place in my heart for the elderly so I said confidently, "Yes, I can!" Although at that moment I didn't have any idea of how I was going to do it.

I quickly altered my own state of consciousness and mentally said, "Help!" to my own higher mind. I immediately got the awareness I needed to proceed.

She told me in response to my questioning that she could borrow her son's cassette player. So I turned on my tape recorder and took her into deep relaxation using a series of routines much the same as I've detailed in earlier chapters. Then my suggestions incorporated these key elements:

1. That she would drift into a deep, completely restful, natural sleep and remain soundly asleep until it was time for her to awaken.

2. That she would awaken whenever she heard my voice directing her to do so, whenever any emergency situation arose that required her to be wide awake and alert, whenever she had had her full complement of needed sleep, or whenever her pre-set alarm clock went off.

3. That regardless of the amount of time she slept, she would always awaken feeling completely rested and full of energy as though she had 8 full hours of perfect, relaxing sleep.

4. That she would listen to this tape recording every night for 30 days, and it would always put her into perfect, restful sleep right away.

5. That at the end of 30 days her mind would be com-

pletely trained, and she was to discontinue using the tape recording.

Then I turned off the tape recorder and allowed her to continue to sleep in my office for another 15 minutes while I did some paperwork.

After 15 minutes, I awakened her. I did *not* turn on the tape recorder for the awakening process; I wanted a tape to put her to sleep, not awaken her.

She awakened completely refreshed and alert. I gave her the tape, and she went home.

A month or so later, she phoned to tell me that she was now off the tape and sleeping well naturally every night.

It worked!

This case illustrates several interesting things. How to improvise on the spur of the moment, and the ability to use your own altered state of consciousness to obtain the information you need in order to handle a situation. I use my own altered state many times every day to tap into my own higher mind for greater awareness. You, too, can develop this ability.

Prostitute Case: A prostitute wanted to give up her profession and get married. She had fallen in love, and she just wanted to become an average housewife and ultimately a mother. Her problem: she did not enjoy sex. In her entire life she had never experienced an orgasm. Sex was always just a mechanical skill for her to use to get whatever she wanted. Now she wanted to change all that. She wanted to experience the enjoyment, but she didn't know how to allow that to happen.

This was one of my most difficult cases. Many things had to be dealt with: poor self-image, negative feelings toward men in general, fear of releasing her toughness and allowing her femininity to emerge, and many other factors.

She prepaid for six sessions. In each session, I had two main purposes.

1. To deal with the self-image, negative feelings about men, etc.

2. To have her visualize performing sexual acts where she would experience pleasure and satisfaction.

During session 1, I had her commit to herself to have sexual relations only with the man she loved. Insofar as I know, this suggestion was immediately successful. I am taking her word for this. She was a compulsive liar also, so I am not able to be absolutely sure. Her visualization of pleasurable sex did not appear to be successful.

A week later at the start of session 2, she reported having had sexual relations every day with her lover, but there had been no enjoyment. During hypnosis, her visualization appeared to produce some physical excitement during mental sex.

Next week at the start of session 3, she reported no pleasure with actual sexual relations. During session 3, her visualization caused a very strong orgasm.

She phoned me the next morning to say that after session 3 she went to her lover and experienced the most profound physical pleasure imaginable.

I never saw her or heard from her after that. She didn't return for her remaining three sessions or request a refund for the unused sessions. I couldn't get in touch with her because she had refused to give me an address or phone number where she could be reached.

I hope the story had a happy ending, but I'll never really know.

Tennis Case: A professional tennis player hit a performance slump and couldn't snap herself out of it. Each time she lost, she sunk into deeper depression. She was to the place where she expected to lose. . .and she did lose. Even players who were far below her skill were beating her. She was the tennis pro at a posh country club, and now was in danger of losing her job because of her constant "duffer" performance. Her serve had become weak, her returns went into the net, she was always in the wrong position and off balance, she had little zip and energy, her moves were sluggish, her timing was off.

I saw her for the first time in a morning appointment. She had a game scheduled that afternoon with a mediocre player. She was sure she would be fired if she lost.

Under hypnosis I had her visualize a perfect tennis game where her timing was perfect, her serve deadly and full of fire, her movements agile and quick, where she anticipated her opponent's every action and was always in exactly the right position. She visualized a game where she did everything 100% right and won without her opponent even scoring one point.

That afternoon she won...just barely...but she won for the first time in many weeks of daily play.

After four hypnosis sessions she was once again soundly beating everyone in sight so there was no need to continue the sessions with me. She had quickly mastered her self-hypnosis, and I am confident that she will never again experience a slump in performance.

Abortion Case: A psychiatric nurse brought her 14 year old daughter to me because the girl was experiencing severe guilt feelings over having had a recent abortion. She had become depressed and withdrawn. She had no faith in herself or in anyone. The boy who had impregnated her deserted her once she became pregnant. Other boys now considered her as an easy score and tried to seduce her.

In reality, she was a lovely, good, worthy young lady who had made one error with a boy under the delusion that she was in love. She didn't deserve this continued punishment she was experiencing.

My job was to get her to forgive herself and to forgive all others and to rebuild her self-image. For the most part, I used the standard techniques found in this book and was quite successful.

The one thing I did in this case that I want to highlight is the use of the **Seashore Trip Routine** found in Chapter 11.

In the Seashore Trip, I had her do four things while she was standing in the sand near the water's edge.

1. I had her write in the sand "I forgive" and then write her own name, the name of her ex-boyfriend, the names of any others who she had felt bitterness toward, and "all others." Then I had her visualize a wave sweeping up over her feet and over the forgiveness message she had written in the sand. When the wave receded, the sand was once again smooth, the message was gone. The message had been carried out into the sea of life where it became a reality. All was truly forgiven.

2. Next I had her write "I love" in the sand followed by her own name, any special names she chose, and "all others." Once again the wave took the message out into sea of life as described in item 1 above. Her love was truly a reality.

3. Then I had her stand on the beach facing the sea. I had her turn to her right and notice an open door on the beach. I told her that to the right was the past, and this was the door to the past. I had her walk over to the door and close it and lock it and throw the key into the sea. She had now closed the door on the past, and could no longer be negatively influenced by the past.

4. Then I had her turn and go to the left up the beach where there was a closed door standing. I told her that to the left was the future, and this was the door to the future. I had her unlock the door and open it, and put the key in her

pocket. I had her gaze through the now open door and see herself beautiful, relaxed, mature, peaceful, and extremely happy. This was her future and she owned the key to it.

The kind of session I have just briefly outlined is extremely powerful and good. I use this type of thing often. Realize, of course, that I have provided just the outline to be followed. You will need to supply the specific set of words to perform this session. By now, you should be confident at being able to do that.

Cut Chin Case: In this case, I was both the operator and the subject. It illustrates how self-hypnosis can be valuable in an emergency.

My wife and I were vacationing at the lake one summer, spending most of our time out on our 18 foot power cruiser. This particular day we had been lying at anchor, and I walked out onto the bow to pull in the anchor so we could get under way. I slipped on the bow and fell, hitting the point of my chin hard on the metal bow rail.

When I pulled myself up into a sitting position, blood was pouring down my chest from my chin.

My wife's face was ashen. "My God!" she screamed, "I can see the bone!"

I immediately pinched the wound shut as hard as I could. As I sat there on the bow, I closed my eyes and almost instantly altered my state of consciousness (in retrospect, I think I probably went all the way down into theta).

I visualized my chin in perfect condition. I bathed it in white healing light and mentally said, "No bleeding. No pain. No scar. No infection. No swelling. Just perfect healing at one thousand times my normal healing rate." I sat there for perhaps five minutes pinching the wound shut, while I remained in an altered state with eyes closed. I maintained the vision of a perfect chin while mentally repeating the words several more times.

Then I brought myself out and opened my eyes. I stopped pinching the wound.

There was no more bleeding. A blood scab had formed. It didn't hurt. My wife wanted to return to shore to cleanse and dress my chin. I said no, that I was OK. We got underway and enjoyed several hours of boating before going ashore.

When I awakened the next morning I found that the blood scab had come off during the night. The only reminder of the accident was a thin, red pencil-like line about an inch long on my chin. Within a week, even this pencil line was gone. No evidence of the accident was left. And at no time was there pain or swelling.

Memory Case: A man phoned me for an appointment to begin a series of sessions for memory improvement. He said he had acute memory failure. Of course, he forgot to show up for his appointment. He phoned again and made another appointment. Again he forgot. This went on for 4 consecutive appointments. I knew if I could ever get him into the office just once, I could give him a post-hypnotic suggestion to return the following week and eventually get him to solve his problem.

So when he phoned again, I had him immediately write a note to remind him of the appointment which I made for 9 am the following morning. I told him to tape it on the glass of the rear view mirror of his car. I stayed on the phone while he did that and returned to confirm to me that he had done it.

This time he showed up for the appointment. After six sessions, for which he was always on time, he had a marvelous memory.

Cut Foot Case: In 1976 a young lady client came in for her appointment on crutches and wearing a cast on her lower left leg and foot. It seems that a couple days previously she was running barefoot in her yard and stepped on something that lacerated the bottom of her foot to the bone from toe to heel. She told me how many stitches the doctor had to put in and that he told her she would be in the cast for at least 3 weeks and perhaps longer, and that she probably wouldn't be able to wear a shoe on that foot for several more weeks after the cast was removed.

She was coming to me for diet control, so I hypnotized her and performed the diet control suggestions. She was one of the most receptive hypnosis subjects I have ever had; I could practically hypnotize her by just saying "Close your eyes and relax." She responded just marvelously.

So before I brought her out, I took her through a procedure and suggestions very similar to what I had done to myself three years earlier when I had cut my chin.

The next week she returned for her next appointment without crutches, without a cast on her leg, and she was wearing high heeled shoes. She took off her left shoe to show me the bottom of her foot. There was a thin, red line from toe to heel and that was all. No swelling or discoloration. The wound was healed.

But this story had a punch line, and she was bursting to tell me. It seems she had gone to her doctor the day after the hypnosis session and insisted that he remove the cast. He refused, and a heated argument ensued. She vowed to take a hammer and break it off herself. To save her potential injury from doing it herself, the doctor reluctantly removed the cast. But he warned her it was at her own risk, was going to cost her more money, etc. She said the look on his face was priceless when he saw a healed foot.

"I don't understand," he muttered.

Then the young lady told him about the hypnosis session.

The doctor became furious. "I thought you had more

sense than to go to quacks!" he scolded. "Obviously, you don't trust me to be your physician. Consider this your last visit to my office. Find yourself another doctor, or should I say find a quack!"

Unruffled, the young lady asked, "Doctor, how do you explain the healing?"

"Obviously, I misdiagnosed it!" he snorted, leaving the examining room.

I've often wondered how you can misdiagnose a lacerated foot.

This case does illustrate very vividly the blind, fanatical opposition that does exist against hypnosis in the minds of some people. People tend to oppose anything they do not understand.

Our role as hypnotists is not to meet these opponents in head to head confrontation, but rather to provide patient, knowledgeable education about hypnosis. And most importantly of all, provide our services with integrity, honesty, and sensitivity. First learn your skill well, then practice it with honor.

CHAPTER 11

SOME ADDITIONAL ROUTINES

This brief chapter contains a few more routines to augment the many routines found in the other chapters. The routines described here tend to be more specialized and can be easily fit into a set of standard routines to achieve a specific purpose.

Seashore Trip Routine
This is one of the most effective routines I have. You will find modified versions of it in chapter 7, *Regression,* and in chapter 10, *Other Case Histories.* It is very flexible and can be used for an endless list of situations. I frequently substitute this routine in place of the **Mountain Trip** routine in session 6 (see chapter 6).

Picture yourself sitting on a large rock outcropping with the sea about 20 feet below. . .notice the roar as the ocean rushes in and hits the rocks below us. . .smell the salt air as the wind gushes against our face. . .notice the contrast between our rocks and the beach.

Notice the sea gulls in the sky above. . .watch them dive for their dinner in the sea below. . .listen to their chatter as they return to the sky. . .notice the other birds around us. . .they show their appreciation for life in their smooth gliding and happy song.

Look behind us and we see a trail to our beach. . .let's walk down that trail to our beach below. . .the smooth path seems to indicate how many people have climbed down from our rock before us. . . these ageless rocks seem to reassure us of the beauty of life, and how, being in harmony with nature seems to give us grace. . .the stones and rocks seem to make a slight set of natural stairs about halfway down. . .now back to the sloping trail. . .the sand is warming up and is so inviting. . .let's take off our shoes and finish our walk to the beach barefooted. . .feel the warm sand squish up between our toes. . .feel the breeze warm us as we reach the beach. . . we are now able to look over the calm sea, glistening to our eyes.

Let's walk toward the water. . .feel the difference of the wet sand from the dry sand we just left. . .bend down and write "I love you". . .and then put the names of our special people we wish to remember. . .now see the sea rush past us, give our ankles a hug, and as it returns, takes our names and our message, "I love you".

Since the hug from the sea felt so good as it took our names and message, bend down again and write "I love you". . .and then put the names of the people you feel you have slighted or hurt. . .now see the wave rush past us, give your ankles a big hug, and as it returns, takes our names and our message, "I love you".

Walk further into the ocean to where the water is about up to your knees and feel the cool reassurance of life. . .now draw in the love of life from this sea. . .up through your feet, until it fills your whole body with excitement and love of life.

Now let's return to the beach. . .pick up that sea shell. . .listen to the message from the shell. . .back on the warm sand. . .turn and look at the sea once more and say "goodby". . .it is time for us to return to our shoes. . .and back up the stairs of life. . .to the top of the rock. We have the love and excitement of life drawn up from the sea within us now. . .say a special thanks to those people who have been thoughtful to you as your sea fades from view.

Balloon Countdown

This routine is nice for group hypnosis, or it can be used for just one person with slight modification. This is also a good routine for children.

Stretch your right arm and left leg and relax. Now stretch your left arm and right leg and relax. Now stretch both arms and both legs. . .all over. . .and relax. Flop your arms and legs into a lazy, comfortable position and close your eyes.

To take a balloon breath, you breathe in through your nose and see a balloon coming toward you. To blow out a balloon breath, you blow out through your mouth and blow the balloon away. And when you get to your favorite place, remember to be very still and quiet.

Now see before you a red balloon. Take a balloon breath; see the red balloon come toward you. Now blow the red balloon away.

See before you an orange balloon. Take a balloon breath; see the orange balloon come toward you. Now blow the orange balloon away.

See a yellow balloon. Take a balloon breath and see the yellow balloon come toward you. Now blow the yellow balloon away.

See a green balloon. Take a balloon breath and see the green balloon come toward you. Now blow the green balloon away.

See a blue balloon. Take a balloon breath and see the blue balloon come toward you. Now blow the blue balloon away.

Now breathe in and see 10. Hold the breath and see 9. Breathe out and see 8. Breathe in and see 7. Hold the breath and see 6. Breathe out and see 5. Breathe in and see 4. Hold the breath and see 3. Breathe out and see 2.

Now see 1 tied to a purple balloon. Grab hold of the 1 and blow yourself away to your favorite place. Your favorite place can be anywhere you want. It can have anything you want in it, because it is your place, your very own place.

Wait for 30 seconds to a minute to allow the subjects to create their favorite place and to explore it. Then continue.

Take a balloon breath and you will feel better. You will relax more in your favorite place. When you want to remember something, take a balloon breath and see the answer behind your eyes. To be in charge of yourself, take a balloon breath. You will do whatever you believe you can do. Give yourself a hug with your elbow for being special people. Now send a warm fuzzy to someone special.

At this point put in whatever suggestions are appropriate for the work your are doing.

To return from your favorite place, take a balloon breath. See a white balloon with your favorite stripes on it. Hold onto the striped balloon and blow yourself back. Now everyone open eyes. Stretch. Feeling fine.

Test Taking

You will be especially calm, relaxed, and confident every time you take a test or examination of any kind. And your brain and eyes will function perfectly when taking any test or exam. Here is how to get an excellent score on every test you take:

First, read the question and answer it if you immediately know the correct answer; if not, do not spend time on it, just go on to the next question. Continue with this method until you have quickly gone over every question on the test once. At this point you will have answered some of the questions. . .just the ones that you immediately knew the correct answer for.

Second, go over each question you didn't answer the first time. Spend a little more time on each question, about one minute. . . no longer. Answer the ones for which an answer comes to mind, then go on to the next question. Continue this way until you have gone over the questions you missed the first time through. You will find that you have picked up a few more answers.

Third, go to any questions that may be still unanswered and mentally ask the teacher for the answer and write down the first thing that comes into your mind. Do this for each remaining unanswered question. This way you will turn in a completed paper and will have a good score.

Migraines

In pre-hypnosis instructions tell your subject to use her self-hypnosis when she feels the first symptoms of a headache, because it is much easier to get rid of it at that point. Once a headache reaches the migraine stage, it becomes very difficult to relax and get fast complete results.

I want you to imagine now that you are looking at a pale blue screen. On the screen is the number 20. See the number 20 on the screen. Now let the 20 disappear, and go deeper. See the number 19, and let it disappear, and go deeper still. See 18, let it disappear. . . 17, and let it disappear. . .16, and let it disappear. A dark blue haze is forming on the screen. . .15. . .14. . .13. . .deeper and darker blue. . . 12. . .11. . .10. . .the screen has now become a deep blue. Take a deep breath now and relax even more and watch your screen turn to purple with a gleaming number 10 on it. Now let the 10 dissolve into the purple, and see number 9 there. Now 8. . .7. . .6. . .your screen is turning green now. . .5. . .4. . .3. . .2. . .1. . .0. Now forget the numbers, forget the screen, and allow yourself to relax even more deeply.

Imagine yourself as you want to be. . .beautiful, free, and relaxed. Feeling good. . .looking wonderful. . .feeling fine. . .full of health. . .full of strength, vitality, and joy. . .free of all pain. . .free of tension. This is you. This is the real you. Every day from now on you will be more and more completely the woman you really want to be. You are just as capable, just as intelligent as anyone, even more so. Whatever needs to be done, you can do it because you are in control. From now on your control will be deeper and stronger all the time because you are relaxed and calm. Because you are relaxed and calm, your head will stay completely relaxed, your neck, spine, all over your body, you will be relaxed and free, and you will not have any more headaches at all. Never again will you have any headaches at all.

You will continue to do your self-hypnosis every day. If you begin to feel the first sign of a headache, you will do your self-hypnosis immediately, and each time you do the little self-hypnosis routine you will relax completely. You will go just as deep as you are now. . .just as deep as you are now. Whatever suggestions you give yourself will go deeper and be stronger every time. Before you go to sleep at night you will do your self-hypnosis routine and give yourself the following suggestion: I will be relaxed and calm. I will sleep beautifully all night long, and when I awaken I will feel just wonderful, and this will prevent a headache from starting at night.

Smoking

I want you to imagine now that you have a cigarette in your hand. See the smoke curling up and getting in your nose. . .it smells terrible. See the smoke curling up from the tobacco and feel it getting into your eyes. It stings your nose and it burns and hurts your eyes. It smells rancid and dirty. It smells just awful. . .filthy and dirty. Now put the tobacco away; you put it down in the ashtray and you walk away. . .away from that dirty, awful, evil smelling smoke. . .glad to be free of that dirty tobacco. From now on you will be completely free of any desire for even a single puff of tobacco in any form. Whenever you think of smoking you will remember that dirty, awful smell and that foul taste, and you will be completely free of the desire for even a single puff of tobacco from now on.

I want you to imagine yourself. See yourself as you want to be. The real you. . .alive, healthy, full of vitality, full of strength, free from your former enslavement to that dirty tobacco. In control of your own behavior, feeling good, able to breathe again, able to smell things again and taste things again. This is you. This is the woman you can and will be. This is the woman you are now becoming. At this very moment you are making a promise to yourself, not a promise to me, a promise to yourself. . .a commitment. . .a commitment that will grow stronger every day. . .a commitment to become the real you and stay completely away from tobacco from now on.

You will remain relaxed and calm. You will feel supremely confident that anything you set your mind to do, you can and will do it. You will be successful and you will enjoy being successful. You will find it very easy to stay completely away from tobacco from now on. Because you will be relaxed and your mouth will be relaxed, you have no need or desire to smoke even a single puff ever again.

Every night you will sleep like a log, and the first thing you know it will be morning and you will awaken feeling on top of the world. The longer you stay away from tobacco, the easier it will be and the better you will feel every day. Whenever you practice your self-hypnosis exercise you will relax completely and very deeply. You will go just as deep as you are now. By practicing your self-hypnosis faithfully every day you will have absolute control over your desire to smoke. You will have the strength to stay away from, and you will stay away from, even the slightest inclination for even a single puff.

CHAPTER 12

SELF-HYPNOSIS

It may seem to be redundant to have a special chapter about self-hypnosis when this entire book is really about self-hypnosis. There are some things that need to be said that are not specifically said elsewhere. The first eleven chapters really bring you the basic knowledge you need to understand and to begin to fully use this powerful tool called self-hypnosis which we will explore in some depth now.

The only significant difference between hypnosis and self-hypnosis is that in hypnosis the operator is one person, and the subject is another person. In self-hypnosis, the operator and the subject are the same person.

If you are fortunate to have a husband, wife, or friend with whom you can share the learning experience of hypnosis, that is great. You can practice with each other using the methods already discussed in this book. This shared learning experience can be extremely valuable for both participants. It draws you closer together mentally and emotionally, and promotes mutual love and respect. It is also easier and faster to learn when you are working in partnership with someone.

Just have your partner hypnotize you similar to the

procedure in Session #2. Then practice the self-hypnosis exercise for a few days. Have your partner again hypnotize you and reinforce the self-hypnosis suggestions. Again practice. How many times you need reinforcement depends entirely on you. If you practice your self-hypnosis routine faithfully every day, probably one or two reinforcements are sufficient. If you can get your partner to take you through an entire six session program as detailed in the earlier chapters, so much the better.

But what about the majority of us who do not have someone to share the hypnosis learning experience jointly with us? What can we do? How do we learn? And most people are only interested in self-hypnosis anyway. . .what about them?

Put aside your concerns. This chapter will bring into focus everything discussed so far, add a few modifications, and show you how to do it easily, effectively, and inexpensively in the quiet solitude of whatever place you choose. . . *all by yourself.*

In Chapter 10, the *Cut Chin Case* showed how I used self-hypnosis for pain control and healing. Other examples throughout the book pretty well convey the idea that self-hypnosis may be nearly limitless in its potential for enriching one's life at every level of life.

You can indeed use self-hypnosis to solve virtually any problem. You can also use it to expand your awareness and to tap into your innate higher intelligence and creative ability. When you use it for this second purpose, hypnosis really becomes meditation. Self-hypnosis can also be used in those moments when you feel the need for the intervention of a higher power into some situation; it then becomes a form of prayer. The subtle differences in these uses of self-hypnosis lies in how you direct your thoughts once you have altered your state of consciousness, i.e., have reached the alpha state. Some expanded uses of self-hypnosis that I call "beyond hypnosis" are discussed in chapter 13. For the moment, we will concern ourselves with the practical, everyday uses.

Here is some fun I had with self-hypnosis. I was scheduled to have two teeth extracted at the dentist's office. The night before, I conditioned myself to control the flow of my blood. The next day I quickly hypnotized myself as soon as I was reclined in the dentist's chair. When the dentist pulled the teeth, I shut off the blood flow from the wound left by the extractions. The dentist was perplexed. He kept saying to his nurse, "He isn't bleeding. Why isn't he bleeding? I don't understand this." I smiled mentally. I couldn't smile physically because of all the tools, cotton and other junk stuffed in my mouth. As an aside, I also visualized fast, complete healing. The wounds were completely healed and the swelling gone within 72 hours; the dentist had predicted one to three weeks.

Here is how one of my clients had fun with self-hypnosis. He was part of a group that was being studied at a local hospital. The doctors were studying dreams. Once a week my client slept overnight in the hospital with an electroencephalograph attached to his head. The electroencephalograph records brain wave activity. By watching it, the doctor can tell whether the brain is in alpha, beta, theta, or delta, and also tell when the sleeper is dreaming and when he is not. The man immediately hypnotized himself as soon as the machine was attached. The machine immediately recorded deep alpha, indicative of sleep or of dreaming. Yet the man was obviously awake. The doctor said, "What the hell is going on here?" Then the man alternately returned to beta, then alpha, then beta, then alpha, etc., and the machine faithfully recorded it. It drove the doctor crazy until the man finally told the doctor what he was doing. The doctor's reply isn't printable.

I have conceived and written nearly all of this book

while in the alpha state. What does this mean? It means you can engage in activity and have your eyes open while still in an altered state of consciousness. Think about this a moment. What a powerful tool self-hypnosis is! It goes far beyond sitting quietly with closed eyes while directing your attention to a goal. To use self-hypnosis in this manner is not easily achievable. It requires a great deal of pre-conditioning while under hypnosis or self-hypnosis. This pre-conditioning would be similar to that for diet control but with completely different suggestions; you will have to devise your own techniques and suggestions for this. Then it requires practice, practice, practice. Take my word for it, the time and effort are well worth the result. Develop your self-discipline and hang in there; you will succeed!

Now, are you hyped up enough to start? Then let us get down to the nitty gritty.

Getting Started

You need some method of programming yourself with directions and suggestions. The first thing that probably comes to mind is to purchase pre-recorded hypnosis tapes that are already on the market and listen to them. Well, yes, that is one solution that will work. I do not have any quarrel with these commercially available hypnosis tapes except that they are usually expensive and they are not tailored to your specific needs and desires; they are necessarily general in nature. For less money than commercial hypnosis tapes, you can purchase your own inexpensive cassette tape recorder and a supply of blank tapes. Then you can make your own "tailored" tapes for your own situation.

This is my first recommendation. If you do not already have a cassette recorder, purchase an inexpensive one. It is only going to be used for voice, not high fidelity, so don't spend a lot of money. I have seen perfectly adequate recorders in discount stores for $15 to $20; there is no need to spend more than about $30. Purchase some inexpensive blank tapes; again, this isn't for high fidelity, so go cheap. Certainly don't pay more than one dollar for one tape.

At this point, your next step depends on your specific desires with self-hypnosis.

Pre-Hypnosis Consultation

Yes, you should consult with yourself before learning to practice self-hypnosis.

This need not be an elaborate procedure, but it is an important one. You should take some paper and a pen and write down the answers to these questions:

1. Why do I want to learn self-hypnosis?
2. What needs can I fill?
3. What benefits can I gain?
4. How can I help others also?
5. What are my goals for self-hypnosis use?
6. Am I dedicated enough to devote 15 minutes a day for the rest of my life to practice this valuable skill?

If you find it very difficult or impossible to answer these questions, it probably means you are not ready for self-hypnosis yet. In this case, just let it rest for a while. You can continue anytime when you become ready.

Usually, what happens if you try to pursue self-hypnosis before you are mentally and spiritually ready is that it doesn't work well for you. Thus, you become discouraged and abandon the idea. Much better, you should wait a while and pursue self-hypnosis when you are ready so you can ensure success.

Most likely you are ready, willing, and able to proceed right now.

Pre-Hypnosis Exercises

Before you begin to actually learn self-hypnosis, there

are several simple conditioning exercises that are beneficial.

Exercise #1: Sit down comfortably and face straight ahead. Roll your eyes upward as far as you can. This is quite uncomfortable. Hold your eyes upward for as long as you can. When the strain is more than you wish to continue enduring, close your eyes and let your eyes return to normal. Sit there with your eyes closed for a minute or two just relaxing and allowing your mind to be as blank as you can.

The benefit is that you have actually forced yourself into a light level of the alpha state. When the eyes roll upward, alpha is triggered. Since alpha is necessary for hypnosis, this exercise begins to train you (and your mind) for entering alpha at will.

Exercise #2: Sit down comfortably and close your eyes. Visualize the letters of your name slowly, one letter at a time. Then visualize your entire name all at once. Then erase your name and open your eyes.

This helps you develop your ability to visualize. Visualization is the key to successful self-hypnosis and to going "beyond hypnosis" as described in the next chapter.

For many, visualization is difficult. Don't be discouraged if you have difficulty. If the first letter of your name is H and you are not able to visualize it, then mentally describe it to yourself. . .two vertical bars with a horizontal bar between them at mid-point. . .like a football goal post. Know in your intellect that the H is there. With practice, you will learn to visualize. As with any worthwhile skill, practice, practice, practice, and more practice makes perfect. This is as true for self-hypnosis as it is for playing a musical instrument. In hypnosis, you are learning to play the instrument of your mind. Whether you remain an amateur or advance to expert, or something in between is entirely up to you and how much devotion, time, and integrity you are willing to invest.

Self-Hypnosis Routines

Case #1: Suppose your only desire is to solve a specific problem—say, diet control—and not primarily to master self-hypnosis. Then just read the diet control sessions from this book into your tape recorder at a pace that is comfortable to you.

After you have recorded Session 1, make yourself comfortable as you play back the recording while letting yourself (via the recording) hypnotize you.

The next day, record Session 2 and then hypnotize yourself with it.

The next day, Session 3, the next day 4, etc. After all six sessions you will have successfully achieved your goal of dealing constructively with the problem, and learning a simple self-hypnosis routine in the process.

You do not have to do these six sessions in six consecutive days. You can space them up to a week apart and still be effective. When the spacing becomes greater than one week between sessions, the residual post-hypnotic suggestions tend to become weak or even ineffective.

For this six session approach to solving a problem, do not do more than one session a day. The mind needs time to absorb and to act upon one session before imposing another session on it.

If your problem is something other than diet, you still use the same method just described, but you tailor it toward your specific problem. There are enough suggestions and examples in this book for you to devise your own modifications. If smoking is the problem, you would say, "I will have no desire for cigarettes," instead of "I have no desire for chocolates." I think you get the idea.

Case #2. Suppose you do not want to deal with a specific problem at the moment. You just want to master self-hypnosis as a skill so you can later deal with any problem or situation you wish when the need arises.

Again, you will use your recorder to hypnotize yourself for the initial training period. Here is what I recommend you record to get started:

1. Record the entire Session 1 and use it on the first day. Add these suggestions to Session 1 at the proper time:

You are now beginning to learn how to hypnotize yourself for any worthwhile purpose you desire.

Every time you hear your voice on tape, you will respond to the directions and suggestions you give more effectively every time.

Every time you practice self-hypnosis, you will be able to do it faster and easier.

Soon you will be able to practice self-hypnosis very effectively without the aid of a recorder, and this is so.

2. On the second day record and use the following:

Routines **A, B, C, D, E, F, G, H** in that order with the following recorded after routine **H:**

You have now learned how to relax your mind and body. In the future, all you need to do to relax your mind and body this much or even more is to close your eyes and mentally count down from 10 to 1, or 5 to 1, or 3 to 1, visualizing each number as you think it.

You are learning the skills of self-hypnosis which you can practice any time, any place, for any worthwhile purpose you choose.

3. On the third day, record and use the following:

Routines **A, B, I, U** in that order with the following recorded after routine **U:**

This room is a very powerful place for you to come to practice your self-hypnosis. You can do anything you wish here. You create your own reality. You can bring anyone into your room you wish simply by asking them in. You can consult or converse with any one here. The resources of universal intelligence are available to you here. You can solve problems, ask questions, practice any skill or speech, shed bad habits, adopt good habits, plan, program goals, seek inspiration and ideas. There is no limit. No limit to what you can achieve in your room. It is your laboratory. It is your magic kingdom. It is your special domain from which you can control your life.

I am now going to stop speaking. Stay in your room for as long as you wish. When you are ready to leave your room, you may count slowly from one to five and open your eyes at the count of five.

NOTE: At this point you should not have anything else on the tape to distract you. Just let the blank tape run; it will automatically shut off at the end. You remain in your room for as long as you wish, doing whatever programming and suggestions you wish, and counting yourself out from one to five when you are finished.

4. On the fourth day, record and use the following:

Sit comfortably in your chair and face straight ahead. Roll your eyes upward and focus your attention on a spot or object in your line of vision that is up high enough to make your eyes uncomfortable, about a forty-five degree upward angle of your eye movement.

Keep your eyes opened and focused on the spot. Take a deep breath, and as you exhale mentally say the number 5 three times.

Now close your eyes and relax.

Take another deep breath, and as you exhale, mentally visualize and say the number 4 three times.

Take another breath, and as you exhale, mentally visualize and say the number 3 three times.

Again take a deep breath and as you exhale, mentally visualize and repeat the number 2 three times.

Once more, a deep breath and visualize and repeat the number 1 three times.

You are now deeply relaxed, and you will continue to relax deeper and deeper with each breath you exhale.

As you continue to relax more and more completely, mentally repeat the following suggestions as I say them:

"I have mastered the skill of self-hypnosis."

"I can use self-hypnosis any time I wish, any place I wish for any worthwhile purpose I desire, and this is so."

"In the future, all I need to do to achieve levels of hypnosis this deep or even deeper is to close my eyes, take a deep breath and slowly count 3 - 2 - 1 as I exhale. At that point, I can program my mind for any purpose I desire. I can go to my private room by simply visualizing my staircase, walking down my stairs, opening my door and entering my room where I can program for any purpose I desire."

5. On the fifth day, record and use:

Close your eyes, take a deep breath and as you exhale, mentally count three and visualize the 3, two and visualize the 2, one and visualize the 1.

Take a deep breath and continue to relax.

Now visualize your staircase. Go down your staircase and enter your room.

Do not speak on the tape for about 10 seconds to allow yourself time to go to your room.

You are in your room now. From now on you can enter self-hypnosis simply by closing your eyes, taking a deep breath, and mentally counting down from 3 to 1 while visualizing the numbers as you say them. At that point, you can do whatever programming or suggestions you wish.

For especially powerful programming and experiences, you can go to your room simply by visualizing your staircase and mentally descending the stairs to your room.

From now on you can awaken whenever you wish simply by desiring to do so and opening your eyes.

You no longer need the tape recording to enter or exit self-hypnosis. You can do it all by yourself whenever you wish. You may use the tape anytime you wish for refresher or for a special programming session that would be easier to do by tape if you choose, but you no longer are dependent on the use of the tape.

I am going to stop talking now. You may open your eyes and awaken whenever you wish.

6. On the sixth day and every day thereafter you do not need a recorder. You can simply close your eyes and do the 3 - 2 - 1 countdown. Then visualize your staircase, descend it, and enter your room. Stay in the room as long as you wish to do your programming and suggestions. Open your eyes when you wish to terminate the session. If you feel you want to awaken more slowly, then count yourself out from 1 to 5, opening your eyes at the count of 5. I use the 1 to 5 count out most of the time because I really go quite deeply into the alpha and theta.

NOTE: In the self-hypnosis sessions just discussed, it is OK to do more than one a day if you wish. Just don't let more than a week lapse between sessions; if you do, I recommend that you start over from the beginning for best results. Also, you may want to refresh yourself by listening to your tapes every once in a while even though you have progressed beyond the point where you have to listen to them. It is kind of like putting a recharge on your battery. You may even want to create new tapes for special purposes.

Case #3. Suppose you don't have, can't afford, or don't want a tape recorder You can still achieve the same results, but it will require much more time and diligence.

You will do all the things exactly as outlined for *Case #2*, but without using a recorder. This means you must memorize everything, and then mentally instruct yourself while relaxing and listening to your mental commands.

This is not simple to do. The part of your mind that gives the memorized instructions tends to want to go to beta level to do so. The part of your mind that wants to respond to the instructions and enter self-hypnosis must go to alpha level to do so.

As a result, your brain frequency tends to vacillate between beta and alpha. This simply means that each session is likely to be less effective than if you had a recorder. Hence, you usually have to repeat these sessions a number of times to achieve results that you would be satisfied with.

But it still will work quite well. You just have to persevere and stick with it.

Uses of Self-Hypnosis

Your subconscious mind is like an obedient servant. It will do whatever it is told. Subconscious does not reason; it just does. If you do not give directions to your subconscious mind, your mind will obey the directions you allow someone else to give it. If you do not establish a good self-image in your mind, and if you allow others to impress upon your mind that you are not a very worthwhile person, then you will become a not very worthwhile person. Why are some boys "Bad boys"? Perhaps it is because parents, teachers, peers, and others verbally chastised them hundreds of times when they expressed themselves in some unacceptable manner by saying, "You are a bad boy!" And the child came to believe it. Think about it. An act may be unacceptable, but that doesn't make the child an unacceptable human being. But the child doesn't know that, so his mind becomes programmed "You are an unacceptable person" and a great deal of human damage has been done.

Fortunately, with hypnosis the human damage can be rectified.

If you have a poor self-image, use your self-hypnosis to change it to what you want.

If you have a habit you wish to rid yourself of. . .smoking, stuttering, lying, or whatever. . .get rid of it with your self-hypnosis.

Improve your skills. Give that speech in your room under self-hypnosis the day before you have to deliver it so you will have it perfected, and you will perform just the way you program yourself to perform.

Go to your room and solve problems. Get information and advice from cosmic intelligence by asking for it. If Mahatma Gandhi is your hero, bring him into your room and ask him what you should do. Sound like science fiction? It isn't. This will be touched on further in the last chapter under *Beyond Hypnosis*.

Get rid of pain. Promote healing. Maintain your health. Live longer and better.

Establish contact with your own higher self. . .your spiritual self. . .your all-knowing self.

Set your goals in your room, and then enjoy life as your mind brings them into reality.

When I was a small child, I knew I wanted two things when I grew up. I wanted a mustache, and I wanted to be a professional writer. I maintained that dream, that image faithfully. I didn't know it then, of course, but I was engaging in *"daydreaming my way to success"*. . .self-hypnosis. I have had the mustache for thirty-seven years now, and I have been a professional writer for twenty-three years. You may not think that was much of a dream, but for a child I think it was quite nice, and the important thing is that it worked. As an adult, I have many other dreams and goals. Some have already materialized. Others are in process, and I can watch the events unfold with childlike excitement.

So, too, can you daydream your way to success through practicing your self-hypnosis faithfully every day. You now know how to do it.

In the next (final) chapter I put a little frosting on the cake, and then you are on your own.

CHAPTER 13

PRACTICAL APPLICATIONS

Up to this point, this book has given you all the data you need to successfully use hypnosis and self-hypnosis for any worthwhile purpose you desire. The book gives you a 100% program for diet control. Instructions were given on how to devise programs for things other than diet control.

But all of you do not want just diet control. Each of you has unique problems and situations. Some of you may not even want to learn a self-hypnosis procedure; you just want a method to handle a specific problem when that problem arises. And even at this point, many of you may be vague on exactly how to devise a program for you specific situation.

Obviously, one book cannot possibly cover the millions of specific situations that exist. However, I will give you detailed instructions for a broad spectrum of situations. From the sampling given in this chapter, you should then see clearly how to do exactly what you want to do.

This chapter covers:
- Several phobias. From these you can construct a program for any phobia.
- Business/work situations.

- Group situations. The buddy system. Hypnosis clubs.
- Uses for the elderly and their families.
- Injury/healing.
- Pain control.
- Consulting with higher authority. This can be a spiritual experience.
- Shut-ins / handicapped / prisoners / bad weather "blahs".
- Habit control.
- Hypnosis at bedtime.
- How you can use the program either with or without the self-hypnosis learning experience.

Buddy System

Some people really prefer to work with someone else rather than work alone. Once in a while a person just doesn't feel comfortable listening to his/her own voice on tape. For people in these two categories, the "buddy system" is recommended.

As far as listening to your own voice on tape is concerned, everyone finds it strange the first few times. But you quickly adjust to it, and you will produce excellent results from your self-recorded hypnosis sessions.

The advantages of working by yourself are:

1. You can do it whenever you wish without having to coordinate your time with a buddy.
2. You can work on those highly personal situations where you would rather not share details with a buddy.

The advantages of working with a buddy are:

1. You don't have to make tape recordings if you don't want to. Your buddy reads the induction to you, and you, in turn, read the induction procedure to your buddy. This gives you experience both as a hyp-

notist and as a subject.

2. Two heads are often better than one in deciding just what approach to use to handle a specific situation.

Whichever you choose—alone or with a buddy—you can achieve excellent results. Most people ultimately use both approaches.

In choosing a buddy, pick someone who is seriously interested in hypnosis and self-improvement just as you are. Pick someone who is sensitive and caring and who is not a blabbermouth who can't wait to spread it all over town that you are using self-hypnosis at age thirty-five to control nocturnal ejaculations.

Your buddy can be a spouse, a family member, friend, business associate, or whatever. It is only important that your buddy be someone you trust and with whom you have a good rapport.

Hypnosis Clubs

A hypnosis club is the ultimate buddy system. Here a group of people with common interests gather to use hypnosis on each other to help each other in some way. It is an immense amount of fun, and you can learn so much, so fast.

I especially recommend hypnosis clubs for the elderly, homemakers, families of the elderly, and high school and college students. The list is by no means limited to these few I have mentioned.

The elderly can help each other gain self-esteem, love, confidence, freedom from pain, more energy and enthusiasm, better mental and physical health, control over stress and depression, and the list continues to whatever else is needed.

Homemakers can help each other eliminate boredom and the daily "blahs". They can help each other breathe life and action into their innate creative abilities, help deal with the spouse and children more effectively, and have greater appreciation of self.

Students can help each other with memory improvement, test taking, developing self-confidence and self-discipline, improving academic and athletic skills, dealing with frustration and confusion.

A hypnosis club can be formal if you wish. You can write up a charter. Develop membership requirements. Perhaps have dues to purchase tapes, books, etc. Establish meeting times and places.

Or the club can be a loose, informal arrangement where six housewives (for example) agree to meet from 2 pm to 4 pm every Tuesday, each week at a different house. Each brings their copy of *Hypnosis* and they alternately become hypnotist and subject as they solve problems. They may even develop new procedures and experiment.

The beautiful thing is that there is no way you can achieve bad results. Nearly always, you achieve what is desired. However, if the subject doesn't cooperate 100%, or if the operator has not yet developed sufficient skill, there just may be no results at all. Remember, this is a learning process that requires much practice, so don't get upset when everything doesn't work out perfectly. There is no way you can cause harm if you follow the guidelines and cautions given elsewhere in this book.

I heartily endorse hypnosis clubs and groups. It is a superb method of mutual self-improvement. You gain by being helped, and you gain by helping others. I would love to see all elderly people, especially, engage in some sort of hypnosis group. There is so much to be gained.

And don't overlook the great opportunity of just having your own family engage in group hypnosis. It is a marvelous way to increase love and understanding within the family.

The one rule I think is necessary for any group, whether a formal club, an informal gathering, or a family group, is sticking to a schedule. You can meet every day if you wish, but you must not be willy-nilly about your meetings. My personal recommendation is to meet at least once a week. Set aside the time and make it happen. Disciplining the mind to produce the miracles you want requires persistence. In no case should you meet less frequently than once every other week because the residual effects of hypnotic suggestion usually wear off in about two weeks. Family groups can probably have frequent meetings because it generally is more convenient for them to get together.

Guard against scheduling a meeting and then cancelling or postponing it. That can become a counterproductive habit which ultimately can give zero results. An occasional rescheduling will be necessary from time to time, and that is OK. Just don't develop the habit of rescheduling, because when you do, you are signaling your mind loud and clear, "My goals aren't very important. Reschedule them", and that is just what your mind will do, reschedule your goals so you won't attain them.

As you can see, hypnosis is more than just a set of words in a relaxing procedure. Much more. It is a way of life, a way of enjoying life to the fullest, a technique for creating and realizing the reality you want for yourself now and in the future. It is a vehicle you can drive through life in. But like all vehicles, it needs a driver. You are the driver. The vehicle will only go where you direct it.

Habit Control
Diet control is one kind of habit control, and that is detailed elsewhere in this book. Other kinds of habit control are: smoking, nail biting, alcohol abuse, drug abuse, grinding your teeth, picking your nose, sloppiness, etc.

Case 1: If you want to control some habit and also learn self-hypnosis at the same time, follow the six sessions detailed for diet control except for two things:

1. Delete all references and suggestions dealing with diet.
2. Add appropriate references and suggestions for dealing with the habit you want to control.

For example, if nail biting is your problem, in Session 2 you would not visualize putting a piece of chocolate in your mouth. Instead you would put your fingernail in your mouth and it would taste horrible. I think you get the idea. Let common sense prevail and you will do just fine.

Case 2: If you already have learned your self-hypnosis procedure from some previous time, then all you need to do to deal with the new habit control problem is;

1. Alter your state of consciousness with your simple self-hypnosis procedure.
2. Give yourself appropriate suggestions for the particular habit. For example (in nail biting):

—I like myself and I am proud of who I am.

—Ugly, stubby, chewed nails are not compatible with who I am.

—When I put my fingers to my mouth to chew, I will immediately remember that I want long, beautiful nails that help enhance my appearance, and I will not bite my nails.

—I am happy I do not bite my nails.

For situations other than nail biting, refer to Chapter 8 for help in devising the suggestions you want to use.

Case 3: If you have not learned the self-hypnosis routine and do not wish to learn it but still want to deal with your habit problem, you can do the following:

1. Record hypnosis routines **A, B, C, D, E, F, I, G, U, V** in that order. (Or you may have a buddy hypnotize you using these routines.)

2. After routine V, record (or have your buddy give you) the suggestions you wish to give yourself. For example, suggestions as in the preceding **Case 2.**

3. Then record, *I will now stop talking for three minutes while you visualize your desired goal.*

4. Then let the recorder continue to run for three minutes without anything being recorded. The purpose here is to allow you time to do visualization of yourself and the goal you desire before more instructions are given to you. In the case of nail biting, you would visualize long, healthy, attractive fingernails, etc. Make the visualization as expansive, complete, and detailed as you wish for the project you are handling. If you think you want more than three minutes for this process, then let the recorder run for whatever longer time you wish. There is no magic number of minutes to visualize; it is your choice. Of course, if you are using the buddy system, your buddy should just say, "I am now going to stop talking for three minutes while you visualize." Then he/she would simply remain silent for the required time before proceeding with the remaining hypnosis instructions.

5. Then record hypnosis routines **W, 1J** (or have your buddy give them to you). In routine **W,** of course, delete references to diet and substitute other appropriate words.

Your finished tape should have the following data on it:

A, B, C, D, E, F, G, I, G, U, V, your specific suggestions for self-help, a blank pause for X number of minutes to allow time for your visualization of success, W, 1J.

6. Then close your eyes and replay the recording, hypnotizing yourself. This step is not necessary if your buddy did the hypnotizing in person.

7. Listen to the tape once every day (more often if you wish) until the desired results are obtained. That is, until you get rid of your unwanted habit. If you are using the buddy system, your buddy would have to do this every day for you. Here is a very clear advantage of making your own tape.

8. If the unwanted habit should start to recur at some future time, get out your tape immediately and use it daily until the problem disappears.

It is rare that you would have to do this more than once after your initial handling of the problem.

For all of the remaining uses described in this chapter, I am going to only give the routines and some suggestions as described in *Case 3* above under the assumption that you are interested in just quickly dealing with a problem by yourself. In all situations, however, you may exercise your own self-hypnosis procedure *(Case 2* above) or a full-blown procedure where you learn self-hypnosis *(Case 1* above). You may use the buddy system also if you wish in any of the following situations.

I want to describe the general approach and some specifics for each situation without laboriously repeating all the routine detail and all the options and variations.

Just become familiar with all the options detailed here under *Habit Control* and those same options apply to all the other situations I will describe next.

Phobias

Agoraphobia: The dictionary defines agoraphobia as "morbid fear of being in an open space." People with this phobia panic when in open places like supermarkets, shopping centers, parks, etc. They usually confine themselves to their home or automobile. In the severe cases, the person will not leave their house at all. Many will leave but only in their car. They will drive someone somewhere, but won't get out of the car themselves. Others will force themselves to make a quick run into a grocery store for a much needed item and get out as quickly as they can; all the time in terror of having a panic attack.

There is no need for these people to continue leading such unhappy lives. Hypnosis can help. They can use the material in this book, or perhaps a friend or loved one will read this book and then help the unhappy phobiac.

A procedure to use is:

1. Record hypnosis routines **A, B, C, D, E, F, I, G, U, V.**

2. Then record the following suggestions (or if you prefer, make up your own):

—I am a worthwhile person, and I am thankful to be alive.

—My Creator gave me the entire world to enjoy and to use for my benefit. This includes small cramped places and it includes large wide open spaces.

—I am now making a commitment to myself to enjoy all of creation, especially all open spaces, large areas, crowds, everything.

—There is no need to fear being in an open or large place because my Creator gave it to me with love to enjoy and use. He never gives me anything that I should ever fear, and this is so.

—I love all of my world, and I intend to use all of it, and enjoy it, and learn from it.

—I give "Thanks" to my Creator for everything He has given me.

3. Then record the following:

I want you to imagine now that you are strolling through a large public park. You are walking alone, but there are other people that you can see walking in the park also. It is a warm, sunny day and you have a smile on your face. You feel great and at peace with the entire world. This is a spacious place. You seem to be able to see forever in all directions. You love it here. You can hear the birds singing in the lush tree tops. Occasionally you meet someone on the path you are walking and they smile and say, "Have a nice day." You smile back and wish them well. What a beautiful place. What a beautiful world. It is not confining you. You can do what ever you want and go in whatever direction you wish. Perfect freedom. You love the spaciousness and enjoy the peace and the experience of being here and of learning all you can about events that take place here. You come to a broad city street and across the street is a large shopping center. You love to shop, and you cross the street and enter the shopping center. It is a huge, roomy place with crowds of shoppers scurrying about. What a delightful place to be. Enter the first shop you come to and browse through all the merchandise there. Pick out some things you like and purchase them. What fun. You love mingling with the people who are having fun just like you. Your smile is so strong that it just may stay on your face permanently. What a beautiful world you live in. Now take your purchases and walk back across the street and into the park again. This has been a perfect outing and you vow to get out more often into the wide open spaces where you can benefit from more of your marvelous world.

NOTE: You can devise your own visualization procedure in place of this one if you prefer. But keep the same concept of enjoying the wide open spaces that your Creator gave you for your benefit.

4. Then record hypnosis routines **W, 1J,** deleting any diet references. Your finished tape should have the following data on it:

A, B, C, D, E, F, I, G, U, V, your specific suggestions for self-help, your visualization instructions, W, 1J.

5. Now close your eyes and replay your tape, hypnotizing yourself.

6. Listen to your tape every day at least once until you no longer have the problem.

7. If the problem should start to recur, start using your tape again until the problem disappears.

Claustrophobia: The dictionary defines claustrophobia as "morbid dread of closed or narrow places". People with this phobia panic when in small, closed, or narrow places. They avoid going into closets. Putting something over their head would send them into panic. Sometimes even a large passenger car is too confining for them.

Like all phobias, these people can be helped through hypnosis.

Follow the exact same procedure as detailed in "Agoraphobia" above except for the specific suggestions and for the visualization instructions.

Some suggestins that can be used are:

—I am a worthwhile person, and I am thankful to be alive.

—My Creator gave me the entire world to enjoy and to use for my benefit. This includes large wide open spaces, and it includes small cramped spaces.

—I am now making a commitment to myself to enjoy all of creation, especially all small, narrow, or cramped spaces, everything.

—There is no need to fear being in small, closed, or tight places because my Creator gave it to me with love to enjoy and use. He never gives me anything that I should ever fear, and this is so.

—I love all of my world, and I intend to use all of it, and enjoy it, and learn from it.

—I give "Thanks" to my Creator for everything He has given me.

Visualization instructions you can record are:

I want you to imagine now that you have just walked into a closet where you store books, magazines, and photographs. The closet has a light in it and you turn it on. This is a tiny closet packed with your private literature. You have come in here to get your favorite book to read so you can spend a quiet, peaceful day reading. A draft blows the closet door shut, locking you inside. At that moment, the phone rings in the living room. You listen to the phone ring and you smile because now you don't have to answer it and have your quiet day interrupted. There is just enough space on the floor to sit comfortably and read. The idea of being locked in really tickles your fancy because now you have a legitimate excuse for not doing anything except enjoy yourself reading, relaxing, browsing through old photographs, and reminiscing. A perfect, quiet, peaceful afternoon with no intrusions from anyone or anything. You love it. You know the key to the door is in your pocket, but you are going to ignore that. Instead you are pretending to be locked in so you can enjoy the solitude of your own private space. Being cramped appeals to you because it brings your friends, the books and photos, close to you where you can feel the warmth of their presence. What a lovely, calm, peaceful way to spend the day. You vow to retreat into your own tiny space in the closet every once in a while so you can enjoy just being with yourself. You hadn't realized before just how cozy and secure this experience could be. You love it.

NOTE: You can devise your own visualization procedure in place of this one if you prefer. But keep the same concept of enjoying the tiny, cramped space that your Creator gave you for your benefit.

Other Phobias: Follow the same pattern as for the two phobias just described. All you need to change are the specific suggestions you give yourself and the visualization instructions you create.

Make your suggestions and visualizations in the same positive vein as I have: giving thanks for what you have and who you are; showing appreciation for yourself; enjoying all situations that have caused you problems in the past. Let your creative mind run free in devising vivid, powerful visualizations and suggestions. There is no limit to what you can achieve if you diligently put your mind to it.

For The Elderly

Many elderly people are beset with a myriad of problems. They have been released from the job market, and they often feel useless. The aging process often leaves them with aches, pains, and physical debilities that frustrate them because it hampers them from enjoying more of life. Their income is limited, often to poverty levels. They want to do constructive work, but have had difficulty in finding anything. Their families are grown and have their own problems, leaving the elderly person to feel abandoned. They crave companionship, but don't know how to find it. Their self-esteem slips, and they become depressed. The list goes on.

There is no reason why anyone of any age should not enjoy life to the fullest. Hypnosis can help.

Follow the same procedure that has been used in the preceding situations in this chapter. That is:

1. Record hypnosis Routines **A, B, C, D, E, F, I, G, U, V.**

2. Then record specific suggestions for the situations you are dealing with. I'll give you some examples shortly.

3. Then record visualization instructions that you create to deal with the specific situation you have in mind. I'll give you one such visualization instruction shortly.

4. Then record hypnosis routines **W, 1J,** deleting any references to diet.

5. Relax and play back your tape recording, hypnotizing yourself.

6. Listen to your tape every day at least once until you no longer have the problem.

7. If the problem should start to recur, start using your

tape again until the problem disappears.

Here are some suggestions you might consider using (refer to Chapter 8 for even more suggestions, or make up your own):

—I am a worthwhile person, and I am thankful to be alive.

—I am happy to be the age I am because I have earned the right by my past daily living and experiences.

—I am delighted to be my present age because I am much wiser and more experienced than I used to be.

—I have many beautiful memories to comfort me at all times.

—There are many worthwhile things that I can do, and I am learning to do more by using my mind to create my reality as I want it to be.

—I command my creative mind to furnish me with ideas and thoughts that will enable me to enrich my life more and more.

—I command my mind to furnish me with the physical fortitude to live each day with ever increasing achievement and enjoyment.

—I thank my Creator for my life and my state of life.

—I ask for the insight to use my innate abilities for greater benefit to myself and others.

—I give "Thanks" to my Creator for everything He has given me.

—I enjoy being with other people, but I also enjoy being alone.

—I am in control of my own life, and I accept responsibility for taking care of myself to the fullest extent of my ability.

One visualization technique you may want to use is the *Seashore Trip Routine* in Chapter 11. This is an especially powerful routine. While you are on the beach, visualize yourself successfully doing anything you enjoy.

I, myself, am a senior citizen. I have no retirement plan because I was cut from the job market before I could retire from anything. The marketplace is not quick to hire older people except occasionally in very low paying jobs. So I took stock of what I can do that has no relationship to age. Here is what I came up with:

1. I am a very good writer.
2. I am an excellent hypnotist.
3. I am a good astrologer.
4. I am a very good lecturer.
5. I love doing all of the above things.

So using my self-hypnosis, I set my goals and brought them into reality. Results:

1. I earn a nice living doing contract writing for various industries.
2. This book is written and published.
3. I have a second book completed and in the hands of a literary agent.
4. A third book is started.
5. I have written, and sold, several articles to national magazines.
6. I give lectures on altered states of consciousness and am rapidly building a reputation and following in this area.
7. I occasionally do astrological consulting work.
8. I recently purchased four villas (on a time-sharing basis) in Cancun, Mexico. So I have a lovely place to vacation several times a year for the rest of my life.
9. I enjoy good health because I programmed it that way with hypnosis.

I have a full life of freedom, enjoyment, and achievement. And it is all because of how I use my altered state of consciousness.

You can do the same or even more. You have at least one ability that you can capitalize on, and most likely much more than that. I only had four major abilities, and I am doing very nicely. You probably have more than four abilities. Start using your head, your altered state of consciousness, your creative mind, and make good things happen for yourself. Don't depend on others. Rely on yourself. You can do it. This book gives you the key, but you must use the key to unlock the door to your own rewarding future.

Families Of The Elderly

Often, family members of an elderly person feel their lifestyle is cramped. Or they feel guilty about not doing more for the elderly member. Or they feel the elderly person is a bother. There are many reasons that family members feel stress. All of these things can be handled successfully with hypnosis.

Use the same general program detailed previously in this chapter.

The hypnosis induction procedures in themselves do a great deal to release tension and stress. In addition, be sure to include good, loving suggestions for yourself and for the elderly person in your family. A few might be:

—I am a worthwhile person, and I am thankful to be alive.

—(Name of the elderly person) is a worthwhile person, and I am thankful to be associated with him (her), and I love him (her).

—I will show my love and appreciation for (name of person) everyday by listening to him (her) more attentively and treating him (her) with more respect and gentleness.

—I will allow (name of person) to be independent and will not try to impose my ideas and desires on him (her).

—I will encourage (name of person) to engage in whatever activity they want that brings them enjoyment and benefit.

These are just a sampling of suggestions. You can come up with more. Chapter 8 has many more to help you.

For visualization, I recommend the *Seashore Trip Routine*. While on the beach, visualize yourself happily engaging in conversation or beneficial activity with the elderly person in question.

Remember, the elderly have a great deal of wisdom and experience to share if you allow it. You benefit from their counsel, and they gain self-esteem from giving it.

Shut-Ins

Shut-ins are those people who are completely or predominently confined to a home or institution. Among these are: people who are bedridden; in wheelchairs or otherwise restricted in their movement; prisoners; those temporarily confined due to bad weather; and even those who are unemployed and have a great deal of time on their hands.

You who are in this group are offered a great opportunity—*time.*

Time can work for you or against you as you choose. This book shows you how to make time work for you. There is no reason for anyone in any situation to not be able to improve their circumstances *if* they choose to do so.

Everyone classified as a shut-in has an abundance of time to devote to self-improvement, and I recommend that you start doing so immediately. Because time is on your side, you have a big advantage over those who have a limited amount of time to devote to self-improvement.

Each of you should definitely give yourself the full blown hypnosis course given in this book. Learn your self-hypnosis technique. Practice many times every day. Become an expert. You can do it in record time because you have *time*.

Here are a few suggestions and visualization ideas to help get you started.

Bedridden: Direct your suggestions toward correcting whatever physical problems you have. Toward improving your self-image. Toward improving your mental attitude. Toward discovering and using your hidden talents; for instance, in bed you certainly can write, paint, operate a telephone answering service, do telephone soliciting, etc., give everything serious thought.

Some suggestions to give yourself:
—I am a worthwhile person, and I am thankful to be alive.
—I am making a commitment to myself to discover and use all the faculties I can muster.
—I direct all my innate healing energies to my (name of the part of your body that is ailing), and I am healing one hundred times faster than normal.
—I enjoy life, and I am learning to enjoy life more and more each day.
—I am triumphing over all obstacles, and this is so.
—I send love to all who have been kind to me.
—I forgive all who have been unkind to me and send them love also.
—I forgive myself for all past transgressions.

Some ideas for visualization are:
—Use the *Seashore Trip* routine to send love and forgiveness and to create a happy, fulfilling future for yourself.
—Visualize yourself actively engaged in successfully performing some work or hobby that you enjoy.
—Visualize yourself happy, energetic and healthy.

Handicapped: Read the preceding section for "Bedridden" because all of that can be applied to you also. In addition, you have additional capabilities over the bedridden because you are probably able to be somewhat mobile. This means an even greater possibility for jobs and hobbies. Exercise your imagination. Use your self-hypnosis to gain the awareness you need to expand your horizons. It really works.

Some additional suggestions you may want to use are:

—I am rapidly overcoming my temporary handicap and learning to live a more fulfilling and rewarding life.

NOTE: I used the word "temporary". Even if your physician or someone else says your condition is permanent, do not accept it as your reality. They have made their best judgement, but you have the right to exercise your best judgement, too. After all, it is *your* life. Use your hypnosis to recognize the reality of your current condition and vow to enjoy life within the constraints of your current condition, but never give in to your current condition. Always strive for improvement. Perhaps some of you will not realize improvement for whatever reason. That is OK as long as you diligently strive for the improvement, because in so doing, you enrich your life in some measure. The only people who fail are those who give up.

Devise your own additional suggestions within the concept I have just outlined.

Some additional visualization ideas are:

—Create your ideal work situation in great detail. See yourself successfully performing. See yourself successfully interacting with others. See yourself doing everything perfectly. Then tell yourself, "This is my new reality, and I command my higher mind to manifest it into the physical world."

Prisoners: Since you are "doing time" make the time

work for you by becoming an expert at self-hypnosis and creating a new, enjoyable life for yourself. To do so requires perseverance and time; make it happen. There are many things you need to address. To mention a few: guilt, forgiveness; attitude; self-esteem; enthusiasm; faith in self; self-control; responsibility; rights of self and rights of others. I think you get the picture.

A few suggestions you may want to consider are:

—I accept responsibility for who I am and for everything I have done and will do in the future.

—I am making a commitment to myself to conduct myself in a responsible manner as a citizen of the Universe.

—I am a worthwhile person, and I am thankful to be alive.

—I intend to use the rest of my life in a peaceful, enjoyable way.

—I vow to myself to act with honor, success, distinction, and integrity in all present and future endeavors.

—I forgive myself for all errors in judgement and behavior and I am determined to do better.

—I forgive all others without reservation for their errors in judgement and behavior.

—I command my higher self to bring me the awareness and ability to create a better life for myself and for others.

Some visualization ideas are:

—Use the *Seashore Trip Routine* to send forgiveness and love. Also use it to close the door to the past and open the door to the future. When you are on the beach facing the sea of life, the door to the past is on your right, and the door to the future is on your left. Go to the door of the past, shut it and lock it, and throw the key into the sea where it cannot be recovered. Then go to your left to the door of the future, unlock it and open it wide, and put the key in your pocket (you hold the key to your future). Look through the door to the future and visualize yourself as you wish to be.

—Visualize yourself shaking the warden's hand and walking away from the prison as a free man.

—Visualize yourself interviewing successfully for a job and getting the job. See yourself performing competently on the job.

—Even while you are still in prison, visualize yourself getting along well with both the other prisoners and with the prison officials. See yourself as a person who is respected by all.

These are just a few ideas. I am sure you can create many more to fit your situation. Good luck!

Bad Weather Blahs: This one is a blessing in disguise. Instead of grumping about being captive at home because of what you perceive as foul weather, be glad for it. First of all, the truth is that all sorts of weather are needed whether you see the need or not. Secondly, the weather gives you an excellent excuse to use the time to your benefit by enriching your life through hypnosis.

Some possible suggestions:

—I am a worthwhile person, and I am glad to be alive to be exactly where I am at this moment.

—I welcome the opportunity to improve my life through self-hypnosis.

—Today's weather is needed for some good reason, and I am glad for it.

You can then engage in self-improvement by giving yourself suggestions for anything you have in mind, be it: improving your Bridge game; improving your relationship with family members or neighbors; seeking a new job; improving health; or whatever.

Your visualizations can be anything already discussed or something new. Let your mind run unfettered. But whatever you visualize, always see yourself happy and successful.

Pain Control

There are three kinds of pain: headaches; persistent chronic pain such as from arthritis or a "nagging" backache; and sharp, usually shorter duration pain such as from a cut, burn, stubbed toe, etc. All of these can be relieved either completely or greatly by hypnosis.

For pain control, I strongly recommend that you first learn your self-hypnosis procedure and practice it daily, even if only for a few minutes every day. That way, when you experience a pain, you can alter your state of consciousness within seconds and deal with the pain.

Here is what the scenario might be if you did not know a self-hypnosis routine and had to rely solely on tape recorded hypnosis procedures.

1. You burn your finger on the stove while cooking. It really hurts.
2. You run to your bedroom to find your tape recorder.
3. Then you search for a blank tape you can use.
4. Then you look for your copy of this book for the induction procedure.
5. Then you record the 10 induction procedures. Then the suggestions for "no pain". Then visualization instructions for perfect healing. Then the 2 closing hypnosis procedures.
6. Then you rewind the tape, sit down, and play it back to hypnotize yourself.

It is a ludicrous scene, is it not? By the time you are ready to deal with the problem, thirty minutes have lapsed. In the meantime, your burn blistered and you had the pain or some discomfort the entire time. Obviously, this is not the most intelligent way to handle this kind of "emergency" pain with hypnosis.

The intelligent way is to already know your hypnosis routine so you can deal with the problem within seconds, avoiding prolonged discomfort. Reread the *Cut Chin Case* elsewhere in this book to see how to deal with this kind of situation.

For non-emergency pain such as arthritis, you can successfully use the traditional tape method we have been discussing in this chapter. After the hypnotic induction, bathe the painful area in your own white healing light and give suggestions:

—No pain. No discomfort at all in my (name of area).

—Perfect healing in my (name of area).

Do the preceding at least daily, or several times a day if necessary to eliminate chronic discomfort.

Headaches are usually best treated as an "emergency" pain and dealt with using your quick self-hypnosis procedure. However, if you have been subject to migranes or frequent headaches, you may want to make up a tape and have it handy if the need arises.

Injury/Healing

The preceding section on "Pain Control" also applies here. I am including a separate section for injury/healing in order to talk about a different aspect. That aspect is: helping others who have pain, injury, or need assistance in healing. Use your hypnosis to help others. If you have a friend who is bedridden while recovering from surgery, go over and hypnotize him/her and give suggestions to ease the discomfort and to promote the healing. Reread the *Cut Foot Case* elsewhere in this book to see how I handled one such case. Of course, only use hypnosis if the person sanctions it;

do not force it on someone.

If you encounter an emergency situation such as an auto accident and medical help has not yet arrived, use hypnosis to make the injured more comfortable. In this case, you don't say "I am going to hypnotize you." Instead, you approach the victim, try to make him comfortable with a blanket or coat. Do not move him because you may cause damage, unless his life is in danger if you don't move him, such as from burning gasoline. Talk confidently and calmly and say, "I will help you relax and feel better until medical help arrives. Just listen to my voice and follow my instructions." Then go through a few brief relaxation procedures and give them suggestions for becoming more comfortable and for having strength to persevere until medical help arrives. This calls for improvising and quick thinking on your part. That is why it is important to become as expert as you can at hypnosis in case you can be of help. Reread how I handled the earache of a young girl elsewhere in this book. That will give you some idea of how to improvise in an emergency.

One note of caution: If you are assisting in a serious accident situation, do not do or say anything to give the victim cause for concern. For example, if the victim says, "I can't feel my right foot. Is it all right?" Do not say something like, "It is practically severed so you probably can't feel it because the nerves are cut." Instead you say, "Don't be concerned about anything. You look OK to me. Let's wait for medical help on these matters. In the meantime, let's concentrate on feeling more relaxed and comfortable."

One more thing, if the victim is bleeding, do what you can to stop the blood flow, all the while talking calmly to relax the person.

Hypnosis is an extremely powerful tool. Learn to use it well for your own benefit and to help others.

Unemployed: Use suggestions from the "Self-Confidence" and the "Work Success" sections of Chapter 8. Visualize yourself successfully interviewing for a job and getting it. See yourself happy and performing well on the job of your choice.

Uses In Business

There is probably no greater use for self-hypnosis than there is in business. Business is plagued with stress, excessive alcohol abuse (probably because of stress), health problems such as heart attacks (probably due to stress), absenteeism, work attitude problems, and mediocre performance by workers. Yet, ironically, business and industry seem to deliberately shun hypnosis as a viable tool. I worked as a technical writer for three different companies that had the problems I just mentioned in epidemic proportions.

In each case I made a presentation to key managers and executives on how hypnosis could effectively reduce or alleviate many of their problems. Since they were already paying me to write, I suggested they allow me to give seminars to teach volunteers how to use self-hypnosis. I offered to deal on a one-to-one basis with problem cases. I would not charge any fee for these services. I would put in the needed extra time on my own.

In each case, I was laughed out of the office. One executive gave polite excuses while fighting to control his laughter. Another was quite nasty. The third just said a loud, defiant "No!"

How shortsighted these men were. Unfortunately, their shortsightedness must have run into other aspects of their decision making also because all three companies went bankrupt shortly after I left them.

If there is one manager, one executive, one person of influence in business reading this book, I implore you to consider its contents in relation to your business. Most of your key problems are people problems, and most can be dealt with effectively through hypnosis. The most successful way to fail is to not take a chance. So be bold and take a chance for the sake of your business and for the sake of all the fine people in your business.

This book gives you all you need to know. There is no need for me to detail additional specific suggestions.

Consulting With Higher Authority

Perhaps the most valuable tool this book offers is the mechanism for consulting with higher authority for guidance and help. By higher authority I mean anyone, living or deceased, who represents higher authority to you. It can be Jesus Christ, Buddha, Krishna, Confucius, Mohandas Gandhi, the prophet Muhammad, Moses, Abraham. It can be a parent, friend, business associate. It can be a president, past or present. It can be literally anyone at all.

For example, if you are an engineer and are wrestling with a difficult engineering problem, you might want to consult with the great inventor Nikola Tesla. If you are a writer and are having difficulty with the novel you are writing, you might want to consult with Harper Lee or some other fine author. A diplomat might want to consult with Benjamin Franklin.

Here is how to do it:

1. Record hypnosis Routines **A, B, C, D, E, F, I, G, U, V.**
2. Replay the tape and allow it to hypnotize you and take you to your own private inner room. (You will be in your room after routine **V** finishes.
3. Stay in your room for as long as you wish. This is where you will do your consulting with higher authority. Don't be concerned about the tape running; it has nothing on it and it will automatically shut off at the end of the reel.

4. While in your room, invite whoever you wish into your room. You can issue your request mentally, but if you prefer, you can speak aloud.

Typically, here is how I do it. After I am in my room I mentally say: "I ask that my friend, consultant, and guide Mohandas Gandhi enter my room and help me. I need your wisdom and counsel at this time."

Then I press a button I have in my room that opens a door through which my guest may enter.

Gandhi enters. Then I talk to him just as I would anyone. I explain my problem or question. I listen for his advice. We communicate. When I have what I need, and if he has no further things to say, I thank him for coming. He leaves and the door closes.

I do all this silently in my mind. However, you can do it aloud if you wish. I find the sound of my voice too distracting, so I speak mentally and sense my guest's reply mentally.

This method works because your higher mind is in direct contact with the higher mind of your guest. For that reason, you could consult with a newborn baby and receive intelligent, valuable information. The baby's higher mind is part of all intelligence, even though the baby's conscious mind has not yet developed.

This whole experience is really a spiritual one, and it is powerful. Gandhi has given me a great deal of valuable help. So have some others I have invited into my room.

Each person has their own unique experience in inviting someone into their room and consulting. Some see the person enter and hear his/her voice (I usually do). Some sense the presence and the information, but do not actually see or hear it (I have had this experience also). Some do not see or sense anything, but they pretend the presence is there and carry on their conversation (I have done this many times). All of these situations are valid and work.

Sometimes you get the information you need right then and there in the room. Other times you seem to get nothing at the moment, but later when you least expect it, the information comes booming into your mind. So don't give up; it works, and it is exciting.

I have had the information I requested come to me while driving my car hours (or even a day or two later) after the session in my room. Always, you should have the guidance you need from some source within 72 hours after consulting with your guest. If not, repeat the consulting session. Persist until you get what you want. Each time it becomes easier and more effective.

Often the guidance you seek can come to you in subtle or strange ways. Here is one personal example to illustrate this. I buy a newspaper only on Wednesday and Sunday because those two issues contain all the ads, a recap of the week's news, the best comics. The other five day's newspapers just aren't worth the bother (for me).

One Sunday evening, I went to my room to consult with Ernest Hemingway. I wanted to quit my current employment and devote my life to writing, lecturing, hypnosis and helping people. I was greatly reluctant to take the chance. I had been with my employer for 18 years. I was an executive with a comfortable salary. To quit for something as nebulous as I envisioned seemed foolhardy. I explained my situation to Hemingway. He said absolutely nothing; he just listened. I thanked him for coming, and he left.

The next morning while driving to work, I had an overpowering urge to purchase a newspaper. The Monday morning paper is the most useless of all daily papers, and here I was buying it on impulse. I browsed through it later at lunch time. Buried in one of the inside pages was one of those little fillers they use to fill up blank space. It said, "There are many excellent ways to achieve failure, but not taking a chance is the most successful."

Those words leaped off the page and told me what I needed to know. I would take a chance and quit my job, and I would be successful at what I wanted to do. So I did, and I am.

I recommend you explore using this great communication path with higher intelligence.

Bedtime

Before I leave this chapter on practical uses for hypnosis, I want to give you just one more very powerful, easy to implement usage. That is going to sleep while listening to a hypnosis tape you have made.

I'm not just talking about using it to help you sleep better—you can use it for that also—I am talking about any purpose you desire.

Your subconscious mind never goes to sleep, nor does your hearing faculties. Therefore, even though you fall asleep while your tape is playing, your mind absorbs everything on the tape and begins the process of making your reality materialize. Of course, while asleep you are in a deep hypnotic state, so the tape works wonders.

Here is all you do:

1. Record hypnosis routines **A, B, C, D, E, F, I, G, U, V** followed by specific suggestions you wish to have become reality.
2. When you lay down to go to sleep, turn on the recorder and drift off to sleep while it plays.
3. The recorder will automatically shut off at the end.

In these bedtime tapes I do not include visualization instructions to deal with the situation, just verbal suggestions. It works quite well.

Suppose you have a job interview scheduled for the next day. Make the tape and put in appropriate suggestions for your success in giving a good interview. You will be calm, speak intelligently, be charming without being gushy, etc. See Chapter 8 for some good interview suggestions.

Then go to sleep while your tape does the work. The next day you will have a fine interview.

CHAPTER 14

THE BEGINNING

This final chapter is titled *The Beginning* because everything up to this point has been to prepare you to begin to enrich your life in whatever manner you choose. This chapter launches you into your new beginning.

Beyond Hypnosis
All through the preceding chapters words like visualization, alpha and theta have appeared. There have been many references to something beyond hypnosis. Many times you have been told your abilities are nearly limitless. There have been strong hints that there are things you can do in addition to the marvelous, exciting things we have already discussed. We have already detailed exactly how you can tailor and reshape your entire life in every respect if you choose to. What more could there possibly be?

If our learning experience were likened to our traditional school system, at this point of your learning experience I would say, "You have just graduated from the first semester of kindergarten!" Reflect on that a moment. You have just learned about one of the most powerful, useful and exciting skills imaginable—and I say that brings you halfway through kindergarten. Then, you must conclude,

163

there must be an awesome amount to experience beyond what we call self-hypnosis.

Indeed, there is an awesome amount to experience, and complete books have been written about it. I just want to open a door in your mind to where you can go beyond hypnosis if you so choose.

Ponder for a moment about where we live, who we are, and what life is all about. We are experiencing life as human beings in just one dimension on a tiny planet in one incredibly vast universe out of many universes. How many dimensions are there? We don't know, but we know there are many. How many universes? Many. When you think about these things, it makes you feel very insignificant. Well, we are insignificant—physically.

But we are really not physical beings. We are merely housed temporarily in a container that we call a body. We are intelligent beings. . .spiritual beings. . .living, eternal energies that always have been and always will be. We are a significant part of the total cosmic intelligence, and as such we have access to any of the information within that cosmic intelligence. Now you don't feel so insignificant any longer, do you?

Well, you should never feel insignificant because you are a participating member of all that is. Be humble, yes. Modest, yes. But never insignificant.

The implications of what I just said are enormous and mind boggling. Did I just imply that somehow you have access to information from other dimensions, from other worlds, from other minds? Yes, that is exactly my implication. It is more than just an implication—it is truth.

How?

You have already made a start with your self-hypnosis.

Visualization. Visualization is the key to success in your self-hypnosis, and to entering the domains beyond hypnosis. The more vividly you can visualize, create and hold mental pictures, the greater becomes your ability to connect with any intelligent experience. You can converse with Gandhi by going to your room, inviting him in, and visualizing him there. Gandhi's temporary house, his body, is dead, but he lives on as an intelligent energy in some dimension, and he is available to you. All intelligent energies are available to you without restriction.

You can go anywhere at a mental intelligence level without your physical body leaving the room. This is astral travel. Visualization helps achieve this. There are other things needed also, as will be discussed shortly.

Alpha. All the things discussed in the first 12 chapters can be achieved by going to the alpha level. . .anywhere in the alpha level. The deeper you go into alpha (lower frequency) the closer you get to theta, and the more profound your experiences become. To go beyond hypnosis, you need to function in the theta level.

Theta. At this level, you are able to experience astral travel, communication with other minds of intelligence sources, tap the resources of universal intelligence, and experience profound enlightenment.

Getting to theta is relatively easy. First, become very skilled at self-hypnosis so you have your mind trained to drop into apha instantly by a mere wish to do so. This will happen for you automatically if you practice self-hypnosis at least 15 minutes every day with integrity; at some point you will just know that all you need to do to go to alpha is to will it so. This is what I do. . .I just will it to be. There are instruments you can buy that will signal you when you reach alpha and theta, but I don't recommend them for two reasons: 1) expensive, and 2) the way I describe in a moment puts you always in control and not dependent on some gadget. My whole thrust is to enable you to be totally self-sufficient and independent.

When you become as skilled at self-hypnosis as I've just described, then program yourself that you will be able to go to theta whenever you enter your room, and then countdown ten to one as you visualize the numbers.

After you have done the ten to one countdown in your room, attempt to retrieve some specific information or make a specific contact. You should have planned the specific project in advance; make it a rather simple project to begin with. If you succeed, you have reached theta. If not, continue programming and trying daily until you ultimately succeed. Sometimes, you will not get your answer immediately. But if you did reach theta, you will receive it within 72 hours.

Once I needed to consult with higher intelligence for some direction in a personal matter. Nothing happened, and I knew I was in theta. The next day while driving my car I was suddenly visited with the intelligence I had sought.

So the key words are: Patience, Perseverance, and Practice.

A Final Word. Literally, the world is your oyster if you want to develop your skills high enough to get it. Go as far as you wish. It is your choice.

Summary

We have examined a great many hypnosis routines. Long ones and short ones. There have been examples of case histories and the routines used. There have been examples of improvising and modifying routines and sequences. You probably have the idea of modifying and improvising pretty well clear in your mind.

I do want to touch on this briefly one more time because it is very important.

1. The hypnosis routines in this book are just some I use. They are good and they work. But there are hundreds of others that work just as well. Each hypnotist develops his

or her own routines and sequences.

2. Use the ones in this book to help you get started and to master your skills. But do not feel locked into them. Feel free to alter, change, or eliminate as you see fit in light of your own increasing knowledge and experience.

3. Improvising is only limited by your own imagination, so use self-hypnosis to expand your own imagination.

4. Use visualization to achieve results. Recall how I had the little girl create a third eye and look at her ear from the inside? Then she lit up her ear like an electric light in a cave. Often the more unusual or bizzare your visualization techniques, the more effective the results. Do not restrict yourself by conventional thinking. Unfetter your mind.

5. The one important caution: Always use positive, constructive statements in your routines and suggestions. Always say what you want, and not what you don't want. For example, you are helping a woman overcome her fear of water by having her visualize herself swimming. You might say something like *"Now visualize yourself wading out into the water. It is warm and relaxing. It is a beautiful day and you are happy. You lean forward in the water and gently stroke your way across the pool. It is a good feeling. You are a good swimmer. . . etc."* Do **not** say something like, *"You won't drown because you are a good swimmer."* Or, *"Don't be afraid, the water isn't deep."* Use of the words *drown* or *afraid* automatically condition the subject to expect the worst, and you will reinforce the fear rather than get rid of it. So think your words through very carefully before using them. Another key word to avoid like the plague is *can't.*

6. Whenever I program for something, I always conclude with: ***"And with harm to no one. . "*** I recommend that you do the same. You don't want to achieve something at a detriment to others or to yourself.

Now you have had the full course. You now possess

knowledge of what is perhaps the most valuable self-enrichment tool in the world today. There is only one thing remaining to do:

Close your eyes, take a deep breath and. . .

STAY IN TOUCH

On the following pages you will find listed, with their current prices, some of the books and tapes now available on related subjects. Your book dealer stocks most of these, and will stock new titles in the Llewellyn series as they become available. We urge your patronage.

However, to obtain our full catalog, to keep informed of new titles as they are released and to benefit from informative articles and helpful news, you are invited to write for our bi-monthly news magazine/catalog. A sample copy is free, and it will continue coming to you at no cost as long as you are an active mail customer. Or you may keep it coming for a full year with a donation of just $2.00 in U.S.A. ($7.00 for Canada & Mexico, $20.00 overseas, first class mail). Many bookstores also have *The Llewellyn New Times* available to their customers. Ask for it.

Stay in touch! In *The Llewellyn New Times'* pages you will find news and reviews of new books, tapes and services, announcements of meetings and seminars, articles helpful to our readers, news of authors, advertising of products and services, special money-making opportunities, and much more.

The Llewellyn New Times
P.O. Box 64383-Dept. 300, St. Paul, MN 55164-0383, U.S.A.

•   •   •

TO ORDER BOOKS AND TAPES

If your book dealer does not have the books and tapes described on the following pages readily available, you may order them direct from the publisher by sending full price in U.S. funds, plus $1.00 for handling and 50¢ each book or item for postage within the United States; outside USA surface mail add $1.00 per item postage and $1.00 per order for handling. Outside USA air mail add $7.00 per item postage and $1.00 per order for handling. MN residents add 6% sales tax.

FOR GROUP STUDY AND PURCHASE

Because there is a great deal of interest in group discussion and study of the subject matter of this book, we feel that we should encourage the adoption and use of this particular book by such groups by offering a special "quantity" price to group leaders or "agents."

Our Special Quantity Price for a minimum order of five copies of HYPNOSIS is $20.85 Cash-With-Order. This price includes postage and handling within the United States. Minnesota residents must add 6% sales tax. For additional quantities, please order in multiples of five. For Canadian and foreign orders, add postage and handling charges as above. Credit Card (VISA, MasterCard, American Express,) Orders are accepted. Charge Card Orders only may be phoned free ($15.00 minimum order) within the U.S.A. by dialing 1-800-THE MOON (in Canada call: 1-800-FOR-SELF). Customer Service calls dial 1-612-291-1970. Mail Orders to:

LLEWELLYN PUBLICATIONS
P.O. Box 64383-Dept. 300 / St. Paul, MN 55164-0383, U.S.A.

Llewellyn's MAGICKAL ALMANAC
Edited by Ray Buckland
The Magickal Almanac examines some of the many forms that Magick can take, allowing the reader a peek behind a veil of secrecy into Egyptian, Enochian, Shamanic, Wiccan and other traditions. The almanac pages for each month provide information important in the many aspects of working Magick: sunrise and sunset, phases of the moon, and festival dates, as well as the tarot card, herb, incense, mineral, color, and name of power (god/goddess/entity) associated with the particular day.

Each month, following the almanac pages, are articles addressing one form of Magick with rituals the reader can easily follow. An indispensable guide for all interested in the Magickal arts, *The Magickal Almanac* features writing by some of the most prominent authors in the field.

State year $9.95

TEA LEAF READING
by William W. Hewitt
This is a fun, how-to book on tea leaf reading. The author teaches you the ancient yet simple mechanics of reading and understanding tea leaf patterns so that you can foresee the future. It is simple and easy to do, requiring no regimen of discipline, no complicated rules or materials to memorize. Everything is included in the book. You just read it and follow its simple steps. The interpretations are even included, so all you have to do is look them up in the extensive glossary.

The philosophy of tea leaf reading is presented in an interesting and clear style in this book, and you are shown how to prepare, analyze and interpret the tea cup. *Tea Leaf Reading* teaches a skill that is easy to learn and master, and one that will give you many hours of fun, camaraderie, and intrigue. Besides that, while you are having fun, you are also expanding your consciousness!

0-87542-308-6, mass market format (forthcoming) $3.95

A PRACTICAL GUIDE TO PAST LIFE REGRESSION
by Florence Wagner McClain

Have you ever felt that there had to be more to life than this? Have you ever met someone and felt an immediate kinship? Have you ever visited a strange place and felt that you had been there before? Have you struggled with frustrations and fears which seem to have no basis in your present life? Are you afraid of death? Have you ever been curious about reincarnation or maybe just interested enough to be skeptical?

This book presents a simple technique which you can use to obtain past life information TODAY. There are no mysterious preparations, no groups to join, no philosophy to which you must adhere. You don't even have to believe in reincarnation. The tools are provided for you to make your own investigations, find your own answers and make your own judgements as to the validity of the information and its usefulness to you.

Whether or not you believe in reincarnation, past life regression remains a powerful and valid tool for self-exploration. Information procured through this procedure can be invaluable for personal growth and inner healing, no matter what its source. Florence McClain's guidebook is an eminently sane and capable guide for those who wish to explore their possible past lives or conduct regressions themselves.

ISBN: 0-87542-510-0   **$6.95**

THE LLEWELLYN ANNUALS

Llewellyn's MOON SIGN BOOK: approximately 400 pages of valuable information on gardening, fishing, weather, stock market forecasts, personal horoscopes, good planting dates, and general instructions for finding the best date to do just about anything! Articles by prominent forecasters and writers in the fields of gardening, astrology, politics, economics and cycles. This special almanac, different from any other, has been published annually since 1906. It's fun, informative and has been a great help to millions in their daily planning.　**State year　$3.95**

Llewellyn's SUN SIGN BOOK: Your personal horoscope for the entire year! All 12 signs are included in one handy book. Also included are political and economic forecasts, special feature articles, and lucky dates for each sign. Monthly horoscopes by a prominent radio and TV astrologer for your personal Sun Sign. Articles on a variety of subjects written by well-known astrologers from around the country. Much more than just a horoscope guide! Entertaining and fun the year round.
State year $3.95

Llewellyn's DAILY PLANETARY GUIDE and ASTROLOGER'S DATE-BOOK: Includes all of the major daily aspects plus their exact times in Eastern and Pacific time zones, lunar phases, signs and voids plus their times, planetary motion, a monthly ephemeris, sunrise and sunset tables, special articles on the planets, signs, aspects, a business guide, planetary hours, rulerships, and much more. Large 5¼ × 8 format for more writing space, spiral bound to lay flat, address and phone listings, time zone conversion chart and blank horoscope chart.　**State year $6.95**

Llewellyn's ASTROLOGICAL CALENDAR: Large wall calendar of 52 pages. Beautiful full color cover and color inside. Includes special feature articles by famous astrologers, introductory information on astrology, Lunar Gardening Guide, celestial phenomena for the year, a blank horoscope chart for your own chart data, and monthly date pages which include aspects, lunar information, planetary motion, ephemeris, personal forecasts, lucky dates, planting and fishing dates, and more. 10 x 13 size. Set in Central time, with conversion table for other time zones worldwide.　**State year $6.95**

THE GODDESS BOOK OF DAYS
by Diane Stein
Diane Stein has created this wonderful guide to the Goddesses and festivals for every day of the year! This beautifully illustrated perpetual datebook will give you a listing for every day of the special Goddesses associated with that date along with plenty of room for writing in your appointments. It is a hardbound book for longevity, and has over 100 illustrations of Goddesses from around the world and from every culture. This is sure to have a special place on your desk. None other like it!
0-87542-758-8, 300 pgs., hardbound, 5¼ x 8, illus.　　　**$12.95**

THE LLEWELLYN PRACTICAL GUIDE
TO CREATIVE VISUALIZATION
by Denning & Phillips

All things you will ever want must have their start in your mind. The average person uses very little of the full creative power that is his, potentially. It's like the power locked in the atom—it's all there, but you have to learn to release it and apply it constructively.

IF YOU CAN SEE IT . . . in your Mind's Eye . . . you will have it! It's true: you can have whatever you want—but there are "laws" to mental creation that must be followed. The power of the mind is not limited to, nor limited by, the material world—Creative Visualization enables Man to reach beyond, into the invisible world of Astral and Spiritual Forces.

Some people apply this innate power without actually knowing what they are doing, and achieve great success and happiness; most people, however, use this same power, again unknowingly, incorrectly, and experience bad luck, failure, or at best unfulfilled life.

This book changes that. Through an easy series of step-by-step, progressive exercises, your mind is applied to bring desire into realization! Wealth, power, success, happiness . . . even psychic powers . . . even what we call magickal power and spiritual attainment . . . all can be yours. You can easily develop this completely natural power, and correctly apply it, for your immediate and practical benefit. Illustrated with unique, "puts-you-into-the-picture" visualization aids.

0-87542-183-0, 304 pgs., 5¼ x 8, illus., softcover   **$7.95**